Here's what these experts have to say about *Road Signs For Success*

"*Road Signs For Success* includes 99, easy-to-read two page inspirational principles. It will help make the rest of your life the best of your life."

— Ken Blanchard
Best-selling Author of *Raving Fans®*,
Gungo Ho!® and *The One Minute Manager®*

• • •

"Jim Whitt has pulled together a marvellous distillation of historical and contemporary wisdom about personal success and achievement. His 99 *Road Signs For Success* describe key natural laws, that once understood and applied, will help anyone realize their dreams."

— Hyrum Smith
Vice-Chairman of FranklinCovey and
Creator of the world renowned Franklin Planner

• • •

"*Road Signs For Success* is a terrific book for motivating oneself and for self-improvement. Jim Whitt has done a masterful job. We in coaching appreciate his efforts."

— Jim Harrick
Coach of the 1995 National Champion UCLA
Men's Basketball Team

Road Signs For Success

ROAD SIGNS FOR SUCCESS®

Copyright © MCMXCIII

First Printing – April, 1993

Second Printing – April, 1994

Third Printing – April, 1995

Fourth Printing – April, 2002

Printed in the United States of America.

Library of Congress Catalog Number: 93-93933

ISBN 0-9636719-0-1

Jim Whitt
Whitt Enterprises LLC
PO Box 700897
Tulsa, OK 74170
800-874-4928 918-494-0009 Fax 918-494-0933
www.WhittEnterprises.com

Published by Dream House Publishers
P.O. Box 2650
Broken Arrow, OK 74012
(918) 251-5454

Contents

Contents continued

Contents continued

Introduction

• • •

You are about to start a journey and this book will serve as your map. You will find 99 "road signs" in its pages. Each road sign contains a principle or a fundamental law that will guide you on your journey. These signs will guide you on the road to reaching your full potential.

You'll find that these same road signs have guided successful people from all walks of life from the beginning of time to the present. These principles were discovered and followed by great philosophers such as Socrates and Ralph Waldo Emerson; great statesmen such as Thomas Jefferson and Winston Churchill; great businessmen such as Thomas Watson and Sam Walton; great athletes such as Satchel Paige and Wayne Gretzky; and great clergymen such as John Wesley and Norman Vincent Peale. These principles have withstood the test of time.

It's been said that success is a journey — not a destination. You will experience a new excitement in your life if you challenge yourself to follow these time-proven principles as you read the pages of this book.

You will discover that ordinary people like you and me can accomplish the extraordinary if we'll simply follow the signs — *Road Signs For Success*.

"An inspired vision can turn your worst nightmare into a dream come true."

— Jim Whitt

• • •

A bank was having "people" problems and I was asked to sit in on an officers' meeting to discuss what the problem might be. It seems that their employees were making "dumb, bone-headed mistakes," according to the president.

I asked if they had a mission statement. Only one to satisfy the regulators I was told. Could any of the officers tell me the mission or vision of the bank? No. This really miffed the president. He told me in no uncertain terms that every employee of the bank knew what the mission was. "What is it?" I asked , "To kiss the customer's lips until they're chapped," snapped the president.

I had to restrain myself from laughing. I doubt that if I interviewed every employee that a single one would have told me that the mission of the bank was to "kiss the customer's lips until they're chapped."

Since we are naturally goal-seeking beings we have to have a goal to set our sights on. In an organization we must establish a vision and values. This enables the employees to match their vision and values with the organization. Without these two critical elements the daily activities of the employees are not going to be in congruence with the vision and values of the organization. The result is inner turmoil — within the organization and the individuals who work there.

If, however, the vision and values of the organization are clearly defined and shared, then employees can match their daily activities to the vision and values. The result — inner peace — for the individuals and the organization.

I use this example in my seminars: Imagine your organization is a vehicle. You're driving and one of your employees taps you on the shoulder and asks, "Where are we going?" "I don't know," you reply. "Besides, it really doesn't matter." We can expect the "dumb, bone -headed mistakes" the bank president described if we don't tell our people where we are going. He just didn't get it. He wasn't getting the results from the employees that he wanted because they didn't know what the mission was. He was expecting them to travel a road with no map or road signs.

I share three "road signs" with the seminar participants that will guide them down the road to organizational success — purpose, principle and perseverance. Purpose establishes the destination. People are not motivated without a purpose. Principle defines values. What values do they esteem as critical to their success? Perseverance — people can overcome the obstacles encountered on their road to success only if they know where they are going.

People problems can be a nightmare — but an inspired vision can turn the worst nightmare into a dream come true.

"Is it the bell that rings, Is it the hammer that rings, Or is it the meeting of the two that rings?"

— Old Japanese Poem

• • •

Independence — it's as American as mom and apple pie. We pride ourselves on being individualists, independent and self-reliant. To achieve individual success, we must be independent but to achieve success as an organization or as a country we must go beyond independence.

Stephen Covey, in his book *The Seven Habits of Highly Effective People*, says that we experience three levels of maturity. Here's my paraphrase of each: (1) Dependence — We are totally dependent from conception through early childhood. (2) Independence — We learn self-reliance. (3) Interdependence — We must learn to cooperate with others.

Dr. W. Edwards Deming, the father of the Japanese industrial revolution describes it like this: "An orchestra is judged by listeners, not so much by illustrious players, but by the way they work together. The conductor, as manager, begets cooperation between the players, as a system, every player to support the others." That's a good example of interdependence — the parts working together for the good of the whole.

If an orchestra is judged by its listeners then a business is judged by its customers, an association by its members and a country by its citizens. And like an orchestra, it is team work, not star performances, that determine how we are judged.

How can we achieve interdependence within an organization? We just need the sense of a goose. By flying in a "V" formation, geese add over 70% flying range as opposed to winging it on their own. The lead goose and each succeeding goose creates an uplift for the bird immediately behind each time they flap their wings. The lead goose rotates back in the formation when it tires and another bird takes its place. And when a bird is wounded or sick, two geese accompany it to the ground until it dies or is able to fly again. That's interdependence.

"Is it the bell that rings, is it the hammer that rings, or is it the meeting of the two that rings? The Liberty Bell is in Philadelphia, the city of brotherly love. It is a symbol of our independence as a nation and a reminder — a reminder that freedom only rings as a result of our interdependence — our ability to work together for the common good. All we need is the sense of a goose.

"Don't part company with your ideals. They are anchors in a storm."

— Arnold Glasgrow

• • •

When we see some of the things that are going on in our country today it's easy to become disgusted and cynical. Congressmen bounce checks on their personal bank accounts and don't pay their tabs at the congressional restaurant. No wonder we can't balance our country's budget and we have a national deficit that staggers the mind. In 1961 we actually had a budget surplus. What happened? Somewhere along the way we parted company with our ideals.

I looked up ideal in the dictionary. One definition particularly got my attention, "a conception of something in its most excellent form." The ideals that this country were founded on were concepts such as self-reliance, free enterprise, the golden rule and pay as you go. Worthy ideals.

We didn't get in the shape we're in overnight. It has taken years, over 200 to be more precise. If we don't like what's going on in Washington we merely have to look in the mirror to point the finger at whom to blame.

It's not that we deliberately set out to part with our ideals. It happened so slowly we didn't even notice. They simply eroded. It's much like a little creek on a farm we owned. That creek used to flow and have water in it all the time. But over the years, beginning back when this part of the country was first being farmed, erosion slowly set in. Wind and rain have washed the dirt into that creek until over the years it began silting in. This process was greatly accelerated during the dust bowl years of the thirties.

Today no water runs at all except after a thunderstorm. Then water will wash down into that old creek bed and pool below a small concrete bridge that was built by the Works Progress Administration in the thirties. And there, after several days, it becomes stagnant. It becomes stagnant because it is no longer moving forward. And that's what happens to us — we become stagnant when we are no longer moving forward. Like the creek that no longer flows, our ideals erode into a state of stagnation.

Don't part company with your ideals. They are anchors in a storm. Let's throw out our anchors. If we do, the storm will pass but our ideals will remain.

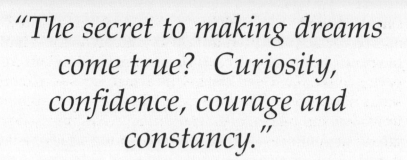

"The secret to making dreams come true? Curiosity, confidence, courage and constancy."

— Walt Disney

• • •

It could be said that Walt Disney lived in a fairy tale world or more accurately created one for us to live in. Even though he has been dead for nearly thirty years we still enjoy the result of his genius. His secret to making dreams come true? Curiosity, confidence, courage and constancy. This twentieth century pioneer shared these same remarkable traits with a pioneer from the fifteenth century, Christopher Columbus.

Curiosity is said to be what killed the cat — but better to die curious than to live in ignorance. Curiosity is what fuels the fire of invention and creativity. Curiosity is natural. As children we ask why — only to be told by adults not to ask so many questions. A few brave souls keep asking however and with their curiosity comes discovery.

Columbus just had to know what lay across the ocean. He suffered a great deal of ridicule in his pursuit and even today, 500 years later, people still miss the point of what he accomplished.

Is confidence a prerequisite for success or is it a result of experiencing success? A little of both I believe. Confidence is like yeast — it causes the bread to rise. Without yeast it goes flat. Confidence is the yeast of ambition. Confidence requires faith in a positive outcome. Why would anyone set sail in three ships for the edge of a flat world? Confidence that it was round.

It isn't enough to have curiosity and confidence. Once you've set sail the obstacles begin to mount and fear sets in. You have to be courageous to look the worst in the eye and not blink. This is where you separate the men from the boys. Columbus risked mutiny and yet kept sailing west.

Constancy should be at the top of the list. In my study of individual and organizational success, purpose is the common thread. Anyone who makes dreams come true has a purpose and remains constant to that purpose. That was true for Columbus, it was true for Walt Disney and it's true for you and me. History holds a place for people with a purpose.

"The secret to making dreams come true? Curiosity, confidence, courage and constancy." In 1492 Columbus sailed the ocean blue — and did something people said couldn't be done. He discovered a new world. Nearly five centuries later Walt Disney used the same formula to do something people said couldn't be done — create a new world. Disneyworld — a place where dreams come true.

"God will not look you over for medals, degrees or diplomas but for scars."

— Elbert Hubbard

• • •

Dr. Viktor Frankl is the author of *Man's Search for Meaning*, a powerful account of his experiences as a prisoner in a Nazi concentration camp during World War II. Dr. Frankl, a psychiatrist, had developed a theory he called logotherapy. At the core of this theory is the belief that man's primary motivational force is his search for meaning.

As a Jew in Austria prior to World War II he saw thousands of German Jews being shipped to concentration camps. He had the opportunity to flee Austria with his wife before the Nazis annexed the country but it meant that he would have to leave his mother and father behind. He also reasoned that if his theory of logotherapy were valid then he must prove it to himself. He elected to remain in Austria.

Eventually he and the rest of his family were incarcerated in concentration camps. Millions died in the gas chambers. He was the sole survivor of his family. The survivors endured suffering that we cannot imagine in our worst nightmares.

It's hard to imagine that anything positive could

come from this morbid experience. But Dr. Frankl did learn something essential to his work. He learned that others may control our lives but they cannot control our attitude. He also learned that the survivors of the death camps were those who had something of importance in their life that made it worth living.

The scars of Dr. Frankl's suffering provided the critical evidence essential to substantiate his theory of logotherapy. Scars are the evidence that the wounds have healed — many patients and fellow psychiatrists have benefitted from his scars.

All of us have experiences in life that wound us. Perhaps, like Dr. Frankl, the scars that come as the result of our wounds and healing will benefit others. In this, there is meaning.

"God will not look you over for medals, degrees or diplomas but for scars." Those scars are reminders that wounds do heal.

"May you live all the days of your life."

— Jonathan Swift

• • •

What's the number one problem faced by Americans today? Is it poverty, prejudice or disease? No, not in my opinion anyway. I believe that life may be too easy. Too easy? Yes — too easy. Why? Because we complain at the most frivolous inconvenience or set back. We have grown soft to the point that we don't remember what true hardship is. Let me give you some examples.

Today we are at peace. Communism has fallen in Europe and is disintegrating rapidly in Cuba and China. Today we have the highest standard of living ever experienced by any nation at any time in history. Today interest rates, inflation and unemployment are at historically low levels. These are but a few examples of what's "right" and yet we complain.

Now for what's wrong. Poverty, prejudice and disease still exist. Businesses still go broke. The economy still has cycles of boom and bust. Politicians are still padding their pockets at the expense of the taxpayer. Elections are dirty, mud slinging spectacles.

My response to what's wrong? Let me answer with these questions. Haven't the things I just listed always existed? Haven't they been as bad or worse than they are today? Won't they always exist to some degree? Yes! Our problem is that we think that the world should be perfect, but problems are a part of life. The world is not perfect nor will it ever be.

We experience life at its fullest when we are encountering and overcoming problems. We pay homage to people in our history books who overcame tremendous problems and persevered — people who lived all the days of their lives. Have we come to believe that life is guaranteed security and perfect health? That would be life in an incubator — it would sustain life but it wouldn't be much fun. Besides, it doesn't exist, it never has and never will. So why do we seek it?

Life consists of good times and bad, health and sickness, boom and bust. ABC Television's Wide World of Sports used to open with video footage of a triumphant athlete, then cut to a snow skier experiencing a bad fall. The audio reminded us of "the thrill of victory and the agony of defeat." It's a reminder that life consists of both. To expect life to be devoid of defeats means it has no victories as well.

Don't expect life to be easy or perfect. Expect the thrills and the agonies — be a competitor in the free enterprise system. Only then can you understand what it means to "live all the days of your life."

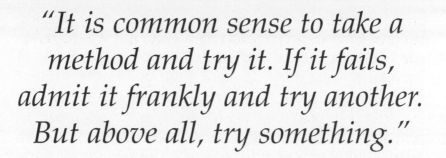

"It is common sense to take a method and try it. If it fails, admit it frankly and try another. But above all, try something."

— Franklin D. Roosevelt

• • •

One summer our air conditioner broke down. The repairman I called operated his business out of his garage behind his house. Like many small businesses he ran his company on a shoestring with very little overhead. There was no receptionist or secretary — he did it all.

Since he was often away from his shop on service calls he utilized an answering machine on his phone. He was hard to reach sometimes but he compensated with an admonition to his customers on the bottom of his business card: "If no answer, keep trying."

I had to laugh when I first read that, but I later thought he had stumbled onto a good philosophy for life. If no answer, keep trying.

One of the most common traits of successful people is that they are persistent. One of the definitions of persistence is, "continuing, especially in the face of opposition." In other words, if there's no answer, keep trying.

When things don't go our way we want to quit. When we have a problem that we can't solve we throw up our hands in disgust and say it's useless. This really is laziness on our part. Elegant solutions rarely present themselves at first.

If our first attempt doesn't work then we have simply increased our odds of succeeding on the next try. Eventually we will fail our way to success. That's how Thomas Edison perfected the light bulb. He just eliminated 10,000 ways that wouldn't work until he found one that did.

Part of the problem is how we view failure. We're afraid of what others might think or say about us. Edison had to put up with this, but remember — it's his name that's in the history books, not the names of those who ridiculed him. We don't remember him for his failures, we remember him for his successes.

"It is common sense to take a method and try it. If it fails, admit it frankly and try another. But above all, try something." The worst sin is not failing, it's not trying.

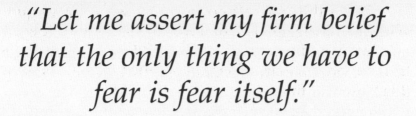

"Let me assert my firm belief that the only thing we have to fear is fear itself."

— Franklin D. Roosevelt

• • •

Why are we so fearful? Self-preservation would be the most logical answer, I suppose. It is a basic instinct that contributes to our survival. From that standpoint fear can actually be positive. But like all good things it can be carried to extremes.

There is a balancing of the scales that takes place in our minds whenever we make decisions in life. On either side of the scales are the cups into which we place the weights of these decisions. On one side is our desire for gain — on the other is our fear of loss. Which side receives the weights that tip the scales? Is it fear or desire?

Movie stuntmen face fear every time they are called upon to execute a difficult stunt such as falling several hundred feet from a building into a small net or jumping through a window while first being set on fire. How do they balance the scales?

Stunt coordinator Gary Hymes best described this in an article entitled "Smash Hits" in the October 5, 1992 issue of *Sports Illustrated*. "A veteran stuntman once told me that fear is a picture you've drawn in your mind of what the outcome is going to be," said Hymes. "It's a perception that you have. If you're afraid of heights, it's because you don't trust yourself to hold on when you're leaning out over the edge of a tall building. Once you understand that, you can change the picture, manipulate it to serve you."

That's probably the best example of how we balance the scales concerning fear of loss or desire for gain. First it depends on how we picture the outcome of our decision. If it's negative then we add weights to the side of fear. Why do we picture a negative outcome? We don't trust ourselves! But we can manipulate the picture and change the outcome in our mind. We add weights to the side of desire — and that means we have to trust ourselves.

"The only thing we have to fear is fear itself." Which way will we balance the scales? How do we picture the outcome of our decision? Do we really trust ourselves enough to place the weights on the side of desire?

A picture may be worth a thousand words but it's value is far greater when it comes to balancing the scales of fear and desire in our minds.

"We hold these truths to be self-evident: that all men are created equal; that they are endowed by their Creator with certain inalienable rights; that among these are life, liberty, and the pursuit of happiness ..."

— Thomas Jefferson

• • •

One virtue that all of us should exercise more extensively is gratitude. It's human nature to focus on what we don't have, what we want and not on what we have to be thankful for. If there is ever a time in history to be truly thankful for what we have it is now.

How about a list to share with your family as you say grace over supper? I'll give you some help:

Nearly fifty years have passed since the last world war.

For the first time in those fifty years the threat of a nuclear holocaust is virtually nonexistent.

Communism is dead in Europe and dying in the rest of the world.

We enjoy a higher standard of living than any generation at any time in history.

We are better educated than any generation in history.

Space travel is old news. We've put men on the moon and launch space shuttles so frequently that it escapes our notice.

Medical science can extend our life by transplanting a heart from a donor. Cancer patients can survive with early detection and treatment — it was certain death not many years before.

We have indoor plumbing, air conditioning and household conveniences such as microwave ovens. We have technological wonders such as computers and fax machines.

More than anything on this list however, those of us in the free world possess opportunity. It is expressed in these words: "that all men are created equal; that they are endowed by their Creator with certain inalienable rights; that among these are life, liberty, and the pursuit of happiness ...."

Just because these truths are self-evident doesn't mean we should take them for granted.

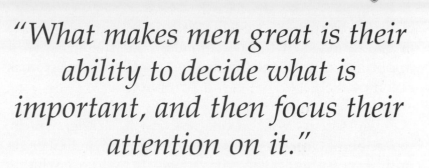

"What makes men great is their ability to decide what is important, and then focus their attention on it."

— Johann Wolfgang Von Goethe

• • •

When asked to explain Britain's wartime policy to Parliament, Prime Minister Winston Churchill responded with, "It is to wage war, by sea, land and air, with all our might and with all the strength that God can give us."

You never had to guess where Winston Churchill was coming from. He was direct. Many considered him to be blunt. He did not leave any doubt as to what he meant. However, his policy was condensed into one sentence — anyone could understand that policy.

Churchill had the ability to cut through all the fat, decide what was important and then get it done. It's a key trait of highly successful people. Unfortunately, many of us get bogged down in the details of unimportant busy work. Things that simply aren't important but consume most of our time.

We could all learn a great deal from Winston Churchill. First, decide what's really important. Discard all excess baggage. Secondly, state what needs to be done in the simplest of terms. Finally, attack what is most important in a relentless fashion, until our mission is accomplished.

Most of us tend to be "reactive." In other words, when there is a crisis we focus our attention on that crisis until it is resolved. The crisis forces us to decide what is important and then act.

We need to be "proactive." That means that we decide what's important instead of letting a crisis dictate that for us. If we were more "proactive" we would be less "reactive." We would discover that there would be fewer crises to manage.

"What makes men great is their ability to decide what's important and then focus their attention on it." We can decide or a crisis will do it for us.

"You see things; and you say, "Why?" But I dream things that never were; and I say, "Why not?"

— George Bernard Shaw

• • •

Most of us have far more ability than we ever give ourselves credit for. How many times have you thought of something innovative only to pre-judge the idea and cast it away as insignificant? Many inventions have been patented by people who were not the originators of their creation — they simply followed through with the idea others had, but dismissed as trivial.

Going through my files one day I ran across many thoughts I considered worthy of coining as quotes — I had written them down and filed them away. Let me share a few with you:

"Coasting through life is fine as long as you're going downhill — but if you're going to climb a mountain then you'd better start your engine."

"Whenever you have an anxiety attack, you need to attack whatever is causing the anxiety."

"It's not that people don't want to, they don't know

how. If we show them how, they want to."

"Until you face your fears you will be a prisoner of them."

"Mediocrity is for the masses — excellence is for the elite."

"You don't have to be perfect to be loved."

"You need to force change instead of letting change force you."

"Success doesn't come to the chosen few — it comes to the few who have chosen."

"Knowing what you're doing isn't a prerequisite for doing what you desire."

"The potential, the rewards and the consequences are all too great for us not to discipline ourselves to take action on the things we must do to succeed."

I've always enjoyed quotes from famous people but never considered myself worthy of coining any. What's the difference between those whose quotes we read and the rest of us? They wrote theirs down, someone published them and we marvel at their ingenuity. Why should yours or mine be published and quoted? As George Bernard Shaw would say, "Why not?"

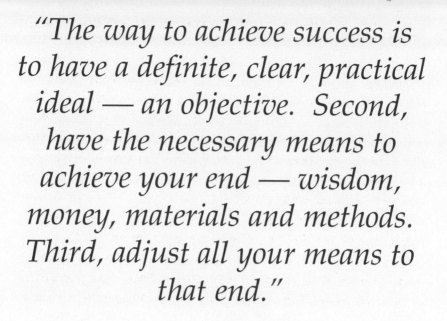

"The way to achieve success is to have a definite, clear, practical ideal — an objective. Second, have the necessary means to achieve your end — wisdom, money, materials and methods. Third, adjust all your means to that end."

— Aristotle

• • •

The vocational educational system in the state of Oklahoma is recognized as one of the best, if not the very best, in the nation. In his book, *Programs for People*, Roy P. Stewart states that all forty-eight states had the opportunity to start programs of vocational education after passage of the Smith-Hughes Act in 1917. But not many have experienced the level of excellence achieved by Oklahoma.

What makes the difference? Why can one segment of the educational system in America shine so brightly when much of the country's educational systems suffer? I think there are two very critical ingredients in their formula for success. In my opinion, it boils down to vision and leadership.

The state of Oklahoma had leaders in vocational education who were visionary people. Visionary people have the ability to look into the future and create in their minds what that future should look like. Those leaders have a vision, it is positive and uplifting. When you share a positive, uplifting vision with people they get excited.

The other ingredient is leadership. Leadership is an intangible trait that's expressed in very tangible ways. Leadership is the ability to gather all the means to that end. People follow leaders because they have a definite goal, they know how to achieve that goal and they enlist others in the pursuit of that goal.

You can see the results of that vision and leadership today. If you walk into an area vo-tech school in Oklahoma you'll find a first class facility with professional, enthusiastic people on the staff.

"The way to achieve success is to have a definite, clear, practical ideal–a goal, an objective. Second, have the necessary means to achieve your end–wisdom, money, materials and methods. Third, adjust all your means to that end."

Vision and leadership.

"The potential, the rewards and the consequences are all too great for us not to discipline ourselves to take action on the things we must do to succeed."

— Jim Whitt

• • •

His record as a college football coach was pretty dismal. In his first eleven seasons he had ten losing records. Then he was fired. He spent the next eighteen years as a coach in the National Football League — fourteen as an assistant, the next four as a head coach. Then he was fired again. At the age of fifty-four, he was hired once again as head coach in the college ranks.

The results? Three years later he coached his team to a perfect winning record and won the national championship. At fifty-seven years of age, Gene Stallings returned the University of Alabama football team to the stature fans had grown accustomed to under the legendary Bear Bryant.

Years of adversity marked his rise to the top. In addition to his setbacks as a coach, Gene Stallings is father to John Mark, who has Down's syndrome. "I think John Mark has made me more tolerant of players with lesser abilities who try hard, and less tolerant of the players with more talent who don't give their best," he said.

Like Stallings, I'm fond of over-achievers, those people who seem to squeeze the most out of the ability they have. On the other hand I think wasted talent is sin. It's kind of like leaving food on our plate after a meal. Remember our mothers telling us that children in China were starving to death and we had the audacity to waste food? That shamed us into cleaning up our plate. Wasted talent is no different. While there are those in the world who are starving to death for the same level of ability that some of us have, we are leaving food on our plate.

There's another lesson to be learned from Gene Stallings' story. At an age when others in his profession are burned out he led his team to a national championship. It's never too late to use the ability and talent that we do have. Unfortunately, most of us are not aware of how much we could achieve. As we grow older we come to the realization that we wasted a lot of our talent in our youth.

It's easy to wistfully look back and think of what might have been. Instead we should take inventory of where we are today and what we can accomplish now. We can learn from our past failings and view them as rungs of the ladder on our climb to reaching our full potential.

The potential, the rewards and the consequences are all too great for us not to discipline ourselves to take action on the things we must do to succeed. What could we do if we really applied ourselves? What are the consequences if we don't? Like mom always told us, people are starving to death in China. How much food is left on your plate?

"Change will either chain you to your past or free you to your future."

— Danielle Kennedy

• • •

Driving down the road in western Oklahoma I came across a scene familiar to this part of the country since the 19th century. Cowhands herding cattle. The scene was different from a few years ago however, the cowhands weren't all cowboys — there was one cowgirl. This used to be an all male ordeal. But in the cattle business just as in the rest of society women have taken their rightful place in tackling jobs that were once dominated by the male sex.

The other thing unusual about the scene was that one cowboy was mounted on a four wheel all-terrain vehicle instead of a horse. Cowgirls and four wheelers. What's the world coming to? Whatever happened to cowboys and horses?

It's answered easily — change. But that's no different than it's ever been. It's just that we measure change within our lifetime. Dr. Norman Vincent Peale's book entitled *This Incredible Century* describes how in his lifetime he witnessed the transition from the horse and buggy as the primary mode of transportation to seeing man set foot on the moon. Talk about change!

When our children were young we had to cross a bridge over a lake on trips to visit my parents. When I was growing up there was no lake. It was simply the Arkansas river. We used to run cattle along the banks of that river. I always pointed out to my children that I used to chase cows on horseback where they saw people water skiing. It's human nature to cling to our past and reminisce about the good old days. But all of the old days weren't so good.

Change brings opportunity. The trouble is that we can't always see the opportunity. We tend to think that the way that it should be is the way that it has always been in our short lifetime. If Henry Ford had subscribed to that philosophy we would still be horseback. Progress marches on — with or without us. The past is like a padlock and change is like a key. When used, it frees us. If not, the lock will rust shut — making us slaves to our past.

"Change will either chain you to your past or free you to your future." Change is the key — but it's up to us to use it.

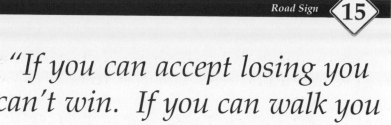

"If you can accept losing you can't win. If you can walk you can run. No one is ever hurt. Hurt is in your mind."

— Vince Lombardi

• • •

In the National Football League the teams that have the potential to reach the playoffs and the ones that actually make it will hinge largely in part on how they handle adversity — injuries, bad breaks, clashes between players and all the other obstacles that fate seemingly creates. Who will make it and who will fold?

The difference between success and failure is how you handle adversity. "Show me someone who's reached the top in any field and I'll show you someone who's had to overcome a lot of adversity," says Lou Holtz, coach of Notre Dame's Fighting Irish.

No one would ever accuse Vince Lombardi of being a sensitive kind of guy — but he got results as the coach of the Green Bay Packers during the 1960's. He led his team to six divisional titles, five National Football League Championships and the first two Super Bowls. Lombardi said that hurt was in your mind — if you can walk you can run. It makes me think of the excuses that we make for not doing something that's a little bit tough or something we don't want to do. Hurt is a form of adversity.

In his book, *Learned Optimism*, Martin Seligman chronicles the results of years of research on a psychological phenomenon called "learned helplessness." Research has proven that we can actually learn to be helpless. Once we encounter some kind of adversity we will learn to overcome it or believe that it is a permanent condition.

All of us suffer from depression to some degree when we encounter adversity. Some people bounce back very quickly, some slowly and some not at all. Seligman says that the difference is our "explanatory style." If we explain our setbacks in temporary terms we tend to bounce back more quickly. If we use permanent terms we tend to stay locked in the chains of depression.

Stuart Smalley, the character on the television program *Saturday Night Live*, lampooned the power of positive self-affirmation when he said with a wimpy lisp, "I'm good enough, I'm smart enough and doggone it people like me." For many years "positive thinking" has been ridiculed as hype. I'm pleased that research now supports the theory that what we say to ourselves determines how we handle adversity. You can talk yourself into feeling good or bad or performing well or poorly.

Ironically, the research on learned helplessness was initiated in the 1960s when Vince Lombardi told his players that hurt was in their minds. Now, research is proving that much of the difference between success and failure is what you say to yourself.

"If you want to be a big company tomorrow, you have to start acting like one today."

— Thomas Watson

• • •

Ray Combs gained fame as the host of the television game show Family Feud. But he only reached celebrity status after years of anonimity.

Ray was a factory worker in Indiana. He had bigger dreams, however. He wanted to be a comedian — he enjoyed entertaining family and friends — making them laugh.

Ray moved his family to California, got a job and posed as his own talent agent. After many rejections he finally landed a job warming up audiences for situation comedies on television. He was on his way but he still had bigger dreams. He wanted to appear on the Johnny Carson program.

Carson's studio happened to be next door to where Ray was performing. Every day after work he would slip into the studio of The Tonight Show. The show was over so it was dark and no one was there. Ray performed his routine just as if there were a live audience. He imagined the audience roaring with laughter. He imagined Carson would be applauding and invite him over to sit with his other guests after he had completed his monologue. He knew this gesture was reserved only for those comedians whom Johnny considered to be really funny.

He continued this routine day after day, week after week. One day a call came from The Tonight Show. Johnny Carson had been backstage one day when Ray was warming up the audience for the sitcom *Amen*. He wanted to know who was responsible for all of the laughs and that's how Ray got his break.

Ray appeared on The Tonight Show and his routine went just as he had imagined — right down to Johnny inviting him over to join his other guests. He acted out his fantasy until it became a reality.

Ray Combs wanted to be a big star in the future so he started acting like one in the present. It works for organizations as well as individuals — we must act like a great company if we are to become one.

We can be what we can see — today's fantasy can be tomorrow's reality. The key is to act as if tomorrow were today.

"Don't be too timid and squeamish about your actions. All life is an experiment. The more experiments you make the better."

— Ralph Waldo Emerson

• • •

We were driving through the pasture to look at our neighbor's cows when we came upon one of them immediately after having a calf. My son was with us and he had never experienced anything like this. The three of us stood nearby and watched as the mother licked and nurtured her baby. The calf was still soaking wet — he'd shake his head and snort to clear his nose of fluid. It's a sight that still brings wonderment to those who have witnessed the process many times.

It occurred to me as we watched mother and calf try to connect for the first meal that life is a series of experiments. The calf would try to stand and then fall down — several times. Then when he could stand he couldn't find his mother's udder. His mother patiently readjusted her stance time and time again. It was a comical scene and it looked like an exercise in futility. But eventually they got it together and the calf nursed for the first time.

Learning is a process of experiments. There are four basic stages that we go through to learn — unnatural, unskilled, skilled and perfection. Unlike the baby calf and its mother we expect perfection the first time. I like what Zig Ziglar says, "Anything worth doing is worth doing poorly, until you can do it right."

In the unnatural stage we don't feel right about the process. We feel like we have two left feet. In the unskilled stage we can do it but not very well. We can do it well in the skilled stage but we have to consciously think about it. Then it becomes natural — it's ingrained as a habit.

Somewhere at a state fair a bull is declared a champion. The proud owner smiles to himself — could this be the same awkward calf that failed so miserably at his first attempts to stand and nurse? He's standing tall today — it's natural.

"Don't be too timid and squeamish about your actions. All life is an experiment. The more experiments you make the better." Champions aren't born — they experiment until they get it right.

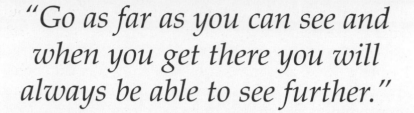
"Go as far as you can see and when you get there you will always be able to see further."

— Zig Ziglar

• • •

We all admire truly successful people — those who have overcome seemingly impossible odds to achieve their dreams. They seem to have an intangible trait that allows them to soar above the masses.

There is another level of people who seem to be "semi-successful." These are the people who attain a certain level of success in life and certainly achieve more than the majority. These people do quite well. They may live in nice homes, drive nice cars, send their children to college and live what we might call a "secure" life. In fact, maybe too secure.

We all naturally strive for security and some level of affluence. For the semi-successful these are their goals and once attained they become their worst enemy. Risk becomes a factor then. Their fundamental physiological needs have been met — shelter, clothing, food and a degree of security. Some of their psychological needs have been met — social acceptance and their self-esteem needs of recognition and a certain level of achievement. But their highest need, self-actualization or the need to realize one's own unique potential may go unmet because of the risk factor.

Highly successful people use the "corridor principle." The future is like a long corridor. There are doors on each side of the corridor but we can't see them until we walk down the corridor. Then the doors become visible. The highly successful apply the corridor principle and risk their needs for security and acceptance. They start down the corridor, even though they can't see the doors from the end, believing there will be doors when they get there. Their willingness to experience the highest degree of risk enables them to experience the highest degree of success.

The semi-successful on the other hand have too much interest in maintaining their current standard of living — it's a death trap called a comfort zone. They, by nature, long for self-actualization but can't quite bring themselves to risk what they have acquired. It's fear of the unknown. As they look down the corridor they can't see any doors so they never start walking; they never take the risk. They remain semi-successful.

There is always another level of success to achieve. It awaits behind a door down the corridor of life. We can only open the door when we are willing to overcome our fear of the unknown and start down the corridor. "Go as far as you can see and when you get there you will always be able to see further."

"First comes thought, then organization of that thought into ideas and plans; then transformation of those plans into reality. The beginning, as you will observe, is in your imagination."

— Napoleon Hill

• • •

Joyce Wycoff's book, *Mindmapping: A Guide to Exploring Creativity and Problem Solving*, describes the relationship between the left and right sides of our brain and how it determines the way we think.

Each hemisphere of the brain is different or is more specialized for specific thought processes. The left side favors these traits: language, logic, numbers, sequence, looks at details, linear, symbolic representation and judgmental. The right side favors these traits: images, rhythm, music, imagination, color, looks at the whole, patterns, emotions and nonjudgmental.

To be creative we must tap into the power of the right side of our brain. Here's an example: I was writing an article on creativity. I had written the first two paragraphs and seemed to be getting nowhere so I gave it up for awhile.

How ironic — to write about creativity and not have any. What an insight — of course I couldn't be creative — I wasn't using the right side of my brain.

Ms. Wycoff describes the creative process in four distinct stages. Preparation, incubation, illumination and implementation. I'll apply them to the dilemma I faced:

Preparation — I'd gathered the material for the message and knew what I wanted to write. Incubation — when it didn't flow I took time out to let my mind rest and gather energy. Illumination — the AHA! The answer struck me as I was totally relaxed. Implementation — armed with the answer, I sat down at my computer and started writing.

This four step process activates the right side of the brain and lets creativity flow. I had completed the first two steps, preparation and incubation — then illumination struck like a bolt of lightning. Implementation came easily once the solution was evident.

Instead of forcing solutions to our problems we need to sit back and relax a little bit — let the problem incubate. Then, our imagination goes to work and "the beginning, as you will observe, is in your imagination."

"I would rather fail my way to success than be a successful failure."

— Winston Churchill

• • •

Success is a relative concept. In other words, what may be successful for one person may not be successful for another.

H.G. Wells, the famous British author defined success like this: "Wealth, notoriety, place and power are no measure of success whatever. The only true measure of success is the ratio between what we might have done and what we might have been on one hand and the thing we made and the thing we made ourselves on the other."

I committed that definition to memory a few years ago and adopted it as my definition of success. I realized that to be successful you must first define success to your own satisfaction. Real success, in my opinion, is what you accomplish compared to how much potential you have.

It's fairly safe to say that most of us are not even coming close to realizing our full potential. One reason is that we set our sights too low — we're afraid to fail so we hedge our bets. Instead of putting all of our chips on the table and rolling the dice we play the odds or play it safe.

We would rather be a "successful failure" than "fail our way to success."

People who accomplish great things set high goals and consequently set themselves up to fail. That doesn't seem to bother them, however. They pick themselves up, dust themselves off and give it another go. Eventually they "fail" their way to success. They become calloused to the ridicule of those who stand on the sidelines and laugh at them.

Winston Churchill was probably no more talented than many of us. He did, however have lofty goals in life. One of them was to become the Prime Minister of Great Britain.

We can set little goals, or no goals at all, and become "successful failures" or we can set big goals and "fail our way to success." It will determine just how close we come to reaching our full potential.

"Things do not happen in this world ... they are brought about."

— Hays

• • •

Sports history was made on September 6, 1991. Mike Powell broke the world long jump record held by Bob Beamon since 1968. A record that stood for 23 years ... a record that has belonged to only four men over the last 56 years. It was a feat that earned him a picture on the front page of *The New York Times* and on the cover of *Sports Illustrated*. It was one of those rare times when man for but a brief moment defies natural law and performs a seemingly superhuman feat.

But that's not the real story. The real story isn't that Powell jumped 29', 4 1/2" or that he set a world record that belonged to Bob Beamon for over 23 years. The real story is that Mike Powell programmed his mind just as we can program a computer.

Powell had started signing autographs for fans with a number in addition to his name. The number was 8.95 — as in 8.95 meters. For those of us who don't think in metric terms that translates into 29', 4 1/2". Each time he signed an autograph he was programming his computer. Like all champions, Mike Powell visualized his record breaking jump immediately prior to his takeoff. In his mind's eye he saw himself go through each precisely calculated move. The real jump was an instant replay of that imagined experience. His jump was exactly 29', 4 1/2" — programmed to a fraction of an inch. Afterwards, while signing an autograph, this time with the number 29', 4 1/2", he remarked that it wasn't even real on paper yet, then added, "Even though my mind told my body it could do it for five years." His body simply followed the instructions that had been programmed into his mind.

Like Mike Powell we possess an "internal computer." One that is infinitely more powerful than the man- made variety. The Creator of our computer has allowed us to program seemingly super-human feats and then perform them. Whenever we witness these feats it should serve as a reminder that we are subject to this phenomenon just as much as any Olympic athlete. We need to ask ourselves, "What are we programming into our computer?" You see, whatever we program in today will determine the results that we experience tomorrow.

"Things do not happen in this world ... they are brought about." They are brought about by what we program in.

"Quality is measured by the difference between our customer's expectations and the product or service we actually provide."

— Jim Whitt

• • •

A new management philosophy swept through America in the 1980s. It was called total quality management (TQM) or continuous quality improvement (CQI).

What is quality? Most people think of quality as statistical processes — measuring variances through control charts or minimizing defects and of course, that is part of quality.

My wife shared this definition of quality in marriage (maybe she was trying to tell me something): "It's the difference between our expectations and reality." That really makes sense. We were driving down the highway during this discussion and I said that is true of quality with anything. "Quality is the difference between our customer's expectations and the product or service we actually provide."

I always take note of how I'm treated as a customer.

Little do the people I do business with realize that they may become the subject of my writings or an example in my presentations (good or bad). I opened an account with a bank the other day and was treated with indifference.

The only reason I selected this bank was convenience — it was close, and their competitors treated me with equal indifference. Maybe all of these banks defined quality in financial performance or in efficiency or productivity but the true measurement of quality wasn't being met — my expectation of service. It was lousy.

Do you suppose a bank that really met the customer's expectations could compete? They could walk away with the lion's share of the market. But no one meets the challenge. Why? Because all the banks in town measure quality by THEIR expectations — NOT the customers!

Quality? TQM? CQI? The litmus test for quality will never be found in zero defects or minimizing variances, important as they might be. We may be meeting or exceeding industry or company standards, but so what? If we want to be known for our quality we only need to meet one set of expectations — the customer's.

"It is necessary to try to surpass oneself always; this occupation ought to last as long as life."

— Christina, Queen of Sweden, 1629-89

• • •

Have you ever noticed that there are certain problems that seem to recur in your life? And these problems are the ones that frustrate you the most — the ones you can't seem to find a solution for?

For example, let's say that you have a problem dealing with a behavioral trait — anger. As much as you want to, you can't seem to get over the hump — you blow up when something or someone frustrates you. Afterwards, you kick yourself and resolve to never let that happen again. Then it happens again.

If you remember the old television program, The Honeymooners, starring Jackie Gleason as Ralph Kramden then you know what I mean. Ralph would lose his temper and threaten to send Alice to the moon. Later in the program, Ralph would repent and apologize.

I believe that when we're faced with these problems there is a lesson to be learned from them. It's just like being in school — if you went to class, did your homework and passed the exams then you were promoted to the next grade. If not, you repeated that class until you earned a passing grade.

Life is a far more demanding instructor— no one has to tell us if we pass or fail — we simply remain stuck at our current social and economic level until we learn the lesson. Once we master the lesson we get to move on to a higher plane of success.

There are certain natural laws or principles that govern our universe. When we act in accordance with these principles we are rewarded. When we violate these principles, justice prevails. Unlike man-made laws the verdict is always unbiased — we get what we deserve.

Once we learn these lessons, however, our work is not completed. We cannot rest on our laurels. There is another lesson to be learned and another promotion to be earned. This process will continue as long as we live.

When that old problem crops up again, ask yourself, "What lesson is to be learned from this?" You can't graduate until you earn a passing grade.

"No pain ... no gain."

— Unknown

• • •

Walk into any weight room and you are likely to see a poster of a musclebound male straining under a barbell with his veins about to burst. The caption reads, "No pain ... no gain." It's the creed bodybuilders live by.

To build a muscle you must first stretch the muscle tissue to the point of tearing. The ruptured tissue then repairs itself and the succeeding levels of scar tissue build layer upon layer until you take the shape of Arnold Swarchzenegger. This is not easy or there would be a lot of Arnold look-alikes.

Developing a team is much like developing a muscle. There are four stages of team growth: Forming, storming, norming and performing. This is outlined in *The Team Handbook* by Joiner Associates.

In the forming stage team members experience anticipation, excitement and apprehension. Teams struggle in the storming stage — they have difficulty agreeing on what needs to accomplished, argue, get frustrated and want to quit. Teams get lined out in the norming stage — they can see the light at the end of the tunnel. Finally they start making progress in the performing stage.

I always tell clients they can expect to go through all

of these stages and I'm sometimes asked if I am being negative by conditioning them for the "storming" stage. I explain that storming is positive. Why? Because the team learns more from struggling with the project than they would if someone simply outlined the desired solution.

Just as with the bodybuilder, resistance builds strength. The team can then tackle any problem because they have experienced and learned the problem solving process. There's no other way to do it except to experience it.

This is true with individual achievement as well as with teams. We learn the most when we struggle — when we meet resistance. We have to move out of our comfort zone and push ourselves — it hurts. When things come too easily we learn nothing. We don't grow. We simply continue down the path of least resistance but remember, resistance builds strength.

At Christmas we celebrate the ultimate example of "storming." Jesus struggled from the time of His birth in a manger until His death upon a cross. We celebrate the glory of His resurrection at Easter. No pain ... no gain.

"Image creates desire. You will what you imagine."

— J.G. Gallimore

• • •

You're riveted to your television screen watching the NBA semifinals. Michael Jordan can't miss! Everything he throws up goes into the basket. Jordan looks at the coach on his way back down the court and shrugs as if to say, "Don't ask me how I'm doing it but I can't do anything wrong tonight." Suddenly Rod Serling appears on the screen to inform you that Michael Jordan has just started his journey into the Twilight Zone.

OK, back to reality — you're really watching a highlight clip on ESPN, the cable sports channel. The subject is "the zone" — that special time in which an athlete is nearly flawless, nearly perfect. By their own admission athletes don't know when they move into "the zone" or when they leave. It seems to be fickle.

Sports psychologists measure the brain waves of these athletes and discover a different pattern when they are in "the zone." It's mysterious or supernatural — or is it? Sports psychologists say that we can train our brain waves. I believe that high achievers in all fields train their brain waves naturally and almost subconsciously. They probably do it especially well sometimes and that is most likely when they enter "the zone."

I believe that these gifted athletes, such as Michael Jordan, only use a percentage of their real potential, just as the rest of us do. But when we're in "the zone" we perform flawlessly or come closer to reaching our full potential.

So what's the formula for staying in "the zone." If we truly do have the ability to train our brain waves then how can we do it? Maybe the key is what we say to ourselves. Studies show that we talk to ourselves but that seventy-five percent of our self-talk is negative and counterproductive. This creates negative pictures in our minds and of course we naturally conform to this picture.

We can change our self-talk — make it positive and productive. This would create a positive picture in our minds for us to conform to. Maybe this is how we train our brain waves — through positive self-talk and visualizing positive outcomes rather than negative.

We may not have the physical gifts of a Michael Jordan but it is safe to say that we, like him, only come close to reaching our potential on rare occasions. Andre Agassi reminded us in his camera commercial that, "Image is everything." He's right of course, but it's our internal image not the external. "Image creates desire. You will what you imagine."

"In life we get what we order."

— Anonymous

• • •

Little Whitney Teeter was asked by her preschool teacher to be the caboose. The class was on a field trip and to keep the troops on track the teacher asked them to pretend they were a train with an engine to lead and a caboose to trail the rest of the make believe cars in between. Whitney told her teacher that she couldn't be the caboose. This perplexed the teacher and she asked why. "Because," Whitney matter of factly replied, "My mommy and daddy have told me that I am a leader."

How powerful are our words? Powerful enough that a little preschool girl has formed her self-image according to the words of her parents. She's a leader — not a caboose. Unfortunately I'm afraid that there are more children being told that they are the caboose rather than the locomotive.

It reminds me of the children's book *The Little Engine That Could*. When faced with the steep hill to climb the Little Engine repeated, "I think I can, I think I can, I think I can."

Jim Harrick is one of the most successful coaches in college basketball. He led the UCLA men's team to a national championship in 1995.

How powerful are our words? Here is what Coach Harrick had to say:

"I tell my players daily that I love them, that if they work real hard they will become the best that they are capable of becoming. In my practices I try to take 'no,' 'not,' and 'never' out of my vocabulary. They are negatives. I say, 'You are too good to keep making the same mistake;' or 'Do it correctly.' When you praise people you will see them open up like flowers and blossom. Believe me, it works. Praise them, praise them, praise them and you will see much better results than you would if you did it in a negative way. Praise works–just try it."

We create self-fulfilling prophesies with our words. We talk to ourselves constantly. What we say depends largely on what we've heard others tell us about ourselves — our parents, employers, friends and others.

"In life we get what we order." Are we a caboose or a locomotive?

"The human race is governed by its imagination."

— Napoleon Bonaparte

• • •

The following are actual quotes from insurance forms describing automobile accidents: "The pedestrian had no idea which direction to go, so I ran over him." Here's another one: "A pedestrian hit me and went under my car."

I'm sure the pedestrians in these cases would say those statements were a matter of perspective. When our emotions are high, our perspective becomes distorted. Our imagination plays tricks on us. It's nearly impossible to remain objective.

During a so-called recession, a friend asked me what I thought about the state of the economy. I told them that times might be tough but there were tremendous opportunities. I asked for his opinion. He told me that he thought we were on the verge of a world depression.

Our imaginations are fed by what we read in the newspaper and what we see on the evening news. My friend who thought that we were on the verge of a depression was an avid television watcher. What did he hear? That we were in a recession and it was getting worse. People were imagining the worst and as Napoleon said, "The human race is governed by its imagination."

I'll be the first to admit that as an individual we can't control the economy. The only thing we can control is ourselves. So why worry about the things we can't control? Let's focus on what we can control — our imaginations, our thoughts, our actions, ourselves.

If the worst comes, so what? Recessions and depressions are nothing new. Life consists of peaks and valleys, good times and bad, war and peace. We have to experience the bad to appreciate the good.

Adversity forces us out of our comfort zones. We become more creative, we work harder, we discover talents and abilities that we never knew we possessed until we were forced to reach down into our souls and call them forth.

Henry Ford once said, "Believe you can or believe you can't — you are right either way." If we are ruled by our imaginations then we have a choice — we can imagine the worst or we can imagine the best — we'll be right either way.

"It is not the neutrals or lukewarms who make history."

— Anonymous

• • •

As a professional speaker, I am the recipient of praise or criticism from audience members. While most feedback is positive, I do occasionally hear from some who just didn't like what I had to say.

This used to bother me until I came to the conclusion that a small percentage wouldn't like my presentation no matter what. In fact, I realized that if some didn't like it then it meant I didn't stand for anything.

Successful speakers are passionate about what they do — they stand for something — their values show through. This is what connects them to an audience — it's known as their "effectual field." This same virtue will antagonize those in the audience who aren't passionate about those same values.

A Chicago inner city drug rehabilitation program was the subject of a television news report one evening. When kids were asked about the key to their successful rehabilitation they stated that they had a "sense of purpose." People who are passionate about their purpose succeed but in the process antagonize others who don't share that same passion. Drug pushers who made big scores at these former addicts' expense now ridicule them. They don't share their sense of purpose.

Rush Limbaugh is the undisputed champion of conservatism. He has the most listened to radio program in America. But he may be the most reviled talk show host in Amercia as well.

Why? He's outrageous, funny, articulate, intelligent and opinionated — but he is passionate. He'll never be accused of being neutral or lukewarm. He has a sense of purpose and his values show through. This, of course, antagonizes those who don't share those values and it provokes their wrath. He takes this all in stride, however, and takes calls on his program from those antagonists as well as those who agree with him. He understands that he will be hated as well as loved. That's the price of purpose and passion.

"It is not the neutrals or lukewarms who make history." History records the deeds of people with a sense of purpose — and who are passionate about it. They are loved — and hated — but never ignored.

"Never, never rest contented with any circle of ideas, but always be certain that a wider one is still possible."

— Richard Jeffries

• • •

Over 100 years ago, James Naismith, an instructor at the Young Men's Christian Association College in Springfield, Massachusetts invented the game of basketball. He wanted to develop an indoor sport for the winter months when football, soccer and other outdoor games could not be played.

He nailed a peach basket to the wall of the gymnasium where his physical education classes were held. Then he divided his class into two teams and started a contest between them. The object of the game was to see which side could toss a soccer ball into the peach basket more often.

After a goal was made, a ladder had to be brought out to retrieve the ball from the peach basket. The game was played, with repeated interruptions to bring out the ladder. Here's the kicker though — this went on for two years until someone figured out they could cut the bottom out of the basket and not have to bring out the ladder.

Two years! Are we really such slaves to tradition that we can't see the obvious? Yes! Ideas have a life span. In other words, something that was a good idea two years ago is not necessarily a good idea today.

Once we repeat a pattern of behavior over and over it becomes our script. James Naismith deviated from his script when he created basketball and yet created a script that no one would deviate from for the next two years. You can imagine the ridicule directed toward the person who suggested the bottom of the peach basket be cut out! Are you kidding? That would destroy the game.

Fortunately the bottom of the basket was removed and the game of basketball evolved into the fast paced, high flying sport it is today. Can you imagine tuning into the NCAA championship game only to see someone trot out with a ladder after each basket was made? It wouldn't sell many tickets.

Never rest contented with any circle of ideas — like the bottom of a peach basket — a wider one is still possible.

"Adversity, if for no other reason, is of benefit, since it is sure to bring a season of sober reflection. Men see clearer at such times. Storms purify the atmosphere."

— H.W. Beecher

• • •

What a difference one day makes. On Monday, December 8, 1941, America was buzzing. Military recruiting offices were flooded with men ranging from age 14 to 72 wanting to enlist. The Friday before had been business as usual.

What happened? Sunday, December 7, had proven to be one of the most tragic days in our nation's history. "A day that will live in infamy," President Franklin Roosevelt would proclaim to a special joint session of Congress as he asked for a declaration of war. The Japanese had bombed Pearl Harbor. Over 2,400 Americans had been killed. The American public demanded justice.

Pearl Harbor marked the beginning of World War II

for the United States. Nazi Germany had been waging war in Europe since 1939. Austria, Czechoslovakia, Poland, and France had already fallen. Britain and Russia were under siege. Europe was on the verge of collapse.

In this country we were divided on the issue of war. There was strong sentiment that we should remain uninvolved. This was known as "isolationism." The attack on Pearl Harbor shattered that theory. We then realized that we could not ignore what was happening in the rest of the world — that when freedom is threatened anywhere that we are at risk as well. Pearl Harbor was the storm that cleared the air. We could see clearly now — the Axis tyrants must be stopped or no nation would be safe.

As individuals we have "Pearl Harbor" experiences. Adversity is never welcome and we take great pains to avoid it. But without fail it causes us to challenge the way we see things. Problems and solutions that were cloudy before become crystal clear. Without adversity we tend to become complacent — we become "isolationists." Adversity motivates us to action.

Pearl Harbor was a tragedy — but who knows what the outcome of World War II would have been had the United States not been motivated to become involved? What would the world look like today?

What a difference one day makes.

"The story of the human race is the story of men and women selling themselves short."

— Abraham Maslow

• • •

Over the Christmas holidays you are bombarded by commercials as you tune into the endless parade of bowl games and television specials. These ads are cleverly designed to eject you from your recliner into your refrigerator. If the product should not appear on your shelf then off to the local convenience store or fast food establishment to fill the need that was so vividly exposed on your screen.

The ensuing result was probably several extra pounds that you vowed to shed as a new year's resolution. Why are we so gullible? Why cave into the desire created by Madison Avenue advertising agencies? Psychologist Abraham Maslow would probably have told us it was to satisfy certain levels in our hierarchy of needs.

According to Maslow, there are five level of needs to be met. The first are the physiological needs of hunger, thirst and sex drive. Second, the need to feel secure, safe and out of danger. Third, the love needs, to affiliate with others, to be accepted and belong. Fourth, the esteem needs to achieve, be competent, gain approval and recognition. Finally, the need to fulfill one's unique potential or what he referred to as self-actualization.

Almost all advertising is aimed at the bottom four — in fact most are at the first level. Ads show us beautiful people eating, drinking, driving certain cars, using certain charge cards and the correlation is that we too, will be beautiful if we do the same.

There are a couple of commercials that appeal to the top level however. "Be all that you can be," and "The Marines are looking for a few good men," were familiar jingles for the armed forces. Will joining the Army or Marines be easy and fun? Not on your life. The underlying theme is, "We'll make you tough. You'll reach your full potential."

Quite a different approach from the chips and beer pitch isn't it? Those commercials appeal to our lowest needs. But we are human, with minds and souls, designed to fulfill our purpose in life. We have a nobler motive.

"The story of the human race is the story of men and women selling themselves short." To be satisfied with the fundamental needs in life is no accomplishment, animals do that. To be truly happy in life we must march continually in search of self-actualization — then as they say in the Army, we can "be all that we can be."

"The worst sorrows in life are not in its losses and misfortunes, but in its fears."

— A.C. Benson

• • •

It's interesting how fear affects us. In a basketball game I attended, I noticed one of the players didn't seem to be himself on the court. I had seen him play many times. He was the team's leading scorer but on this night he was tentative and hesitant.

After the game he admitted he was afraid he would miss when he shot. Why would the leading scorer be fearful of missing? "Because the coach chews me out when I miss," he replied. Fear of criticism caused him to freeze up.

Fear will cause us to do that. Denis Waitley says that we are constantly moving toward our most dominant thought. Therefore, if fear occupies our mind we are constantly moving toward what we fear. Rather than avoiding what we fear, we bring it to pass.

When Franklin Roosevelt was elected President in 1932 our nation was in the depths of the Great Depression. Conditions were so bad that during his inaugural address the militia had mounted machine guns on surrounding buildings in case of a riot. It never happened. Instead, FDR made famous this statement in his address that day, "The only thing we have to fear is fear itself." Fear of the depression was a more formidable enemy than the depression itself.

Today there are those proclaiming gloom and doom. The more we hear it the more fearful we become. We become tentative and hesitant. We start becoming concerned about making mistakes — so we freeze. We think that by doing nothing we will avoid what we fear. Will Rogers once said, "Even if you are on the right track you can still get run over if you just sit there."

There are still opportunities if we don't just sit there. During the Great Depression businesses were started and people became wealthy. H.L. Hunt, the billionaire oil man, was a broke cotton farmer in the 1930s. At the time of his death his income was estimated to be between three and five million dollars a day.

Dr. Carl Menninger said that if fears can be learned, then they can be unlearned. We'll discover what we feared didn't happen or even if it did we were able to accept it or overcome it. Only then will we realize — the only thing we had to fear was fear itself.

"Adversity is not bad — it's inconvenient, uncomfortable and sometimes painful — but it's the most powerful catalyst for positive change and growth."

— Jim Whitt

• • •

It seems as though when we are going through some really tough battle that there can be no good in it.

In 1992 we witnessed the homecoming of many hostages from the Middle East. I was always amazed at their attitudes upon their release. It seemed that they all came back stronger and with more moral conviction. They talked openly about their "faith."

One of my favorite stories from the Bible is about the hostage named Joseph. Joseph was sold into slavery by his brothers. He found favor with his master but was framed for a crime he didn't commit and jailed. He found favor with the jailer and eventually was given a "chance" as the result of an encounter with a fellow prisoner.

The end result? He became the most powerful man not only in Egypt but the world.

Napoleon Hill states in his best seller, *Think and Grow Rich*, that the seed of an equal or greater benefit lies in every adversity. If we buy into this philosophy then we simply have to start looking for that benefit. Joseph didn't focus on the adversity, he focused on the benefit.

The truth is that we lose our ability to be objective about adversity. Adversity is like a wall. We must figure out how to go over, around, under or through the wall. If we don't we become frustrated and that results in stress. Stress further distorts our perception and we become more frustrated.

Adversity forces us out of our comfort zone and we don't like that. But it is when we get out of our comfort zone that we grow and become better people. We discover abilities that we never knew we possessed. All of a sudden, the adversity has passed — and we are left only with the benefit. The pain and anxiety are forgotten.

Adversity is not bad — it's inconvenient, uncomfortable and sometimes painful — but it's the most powerful catalyst for positive change and growth. Look at it this way — if Joseph hadn't been sold into slavery, he would have just been another sheepherder from back home.

"You don't skate to where the puck has been, you skate to where the puck will be."

— Wayne Gretzky

• • •

Hockey star Wayne Gretzky is commonly called the "Great Gretzky." What makes him great? It might be that he has a knack for knowing where the puck will be, finding it, and scoring when he gets it. Gretzky understands that if you skate to where the puck has been, you'll likely be left watching someone else skating away with it.

One of our basic fears is fear of the unknown. The "unknown" resides in the future so we typically tend to make decisions based on what's known. The problem is that the "known" resides in the past so we tend to skate to where the puck has been rather than where it will be. Even if the "known" is uncomfortable we will usually cling to it rather than risk the unknown future.

I have a simple formula that puts the past, present and future in perspective. It goes like this, "Reflect on the past, visualize the future and act today."

We want to reflect on the past. Learn from past successes and failures. But to believe that the past holds all the answers to the future will cause us to skate to where the puck has been.

We want to visualize our future. Successful individuals and organizations are purpose driven. They know where they want to go. Like Gretzky, they develop a knack for knowing where the puck will be. "Having a positive vision of the future is the most powerful motivation for change that we possess," according to futurist Joel Barker.

We want to act today. Even if you know where the puck will be you have to start skating now. We've all seen great strategic plans that died stillborn because they collected dust on a shelf.

We live in a rapidly changing world. Jobs and whole industries become obsolete or change form to where they are barely recognizable seemingly overnight. "You don't skate to where the puck has been, you skate to where the puck will be." Reflect on the past, visualize the future and act today.

"Life ain't in holding good cards but in playing a bad hand well."

— P.L. Gassaway

• • •

I spent some time in Las Vegas while I was there for a speaking engagement. I may have set a record — I was there for two days and never gambled a penny. I fully intended to but I got to thinking — I own a business — do I really need to go to Las Vegas to gamble? Like you I roll the dice every day — life is a gamble.

As I observed thousands of people playing black jack or poker, I wondered what motivated them — who were the winners — why did they win? Who were the losers — why did they lose?

Everyone is dealt cards from the same deck so you know that on the average a person is going to get some good hands and some bad hands. The key to winning over the long haul is not getting great hands every time — averages won't allow that. The key to winning is playing the bad hands as well as you can.

P.L. Gassaway was my grandfather. He was born to a circuit riding Methodist preacher before the turn of the century and like many in the ministry they were poor. He only received a second grade education but went on to become a United States Congressman. He was dealt a bad hand but he played it well.

Some people complain about the hand they are dealt. Instead of putting their chips on the table they make excuses for not winning. Others take a hard look at their cards — they know that if they "stick it out" they'll eventually get their share of good hands and when they do they make their move. They look for opportunities.

That's basically the difference between winners and losers — winners look for ways to win — losers look for excuses to lose.

How do we develop a winner's attitude? First we have to accept the fact that we have to play the hand we're dealt without complaining — there is nothing we can do about that. Next, figure the odds — odds are that if we stick with it the law of averages will work in our favor. Finally, refuse to quit — stay with it until good things start to happen — and eventually they will.

"Life ain't in holding good cards but in playing a bad hand well." It's more a case of being a good player than a case of holding good cards.

"There are two ways of exerting one's strength: one is pushing down, the other is pulling up."

— Booker T. Washington

• • •

If a company wants employees to treat the customer well then it must do the same for its employees. In an authoritarian management culture, employees are repressed and they respond in kind to the customer. In a participative management culture, the employees are empowered and they, likewise, respond in kind to the customer. The culture is easily distinguished by the customer.

I like to fly Southwest Airlines. Why? Because of the inexpensive fares? They are among the most competitive in the markets they serve but the reason I like Southwest is their people. Their flight attendants love their jobs and it shows. Their reservation agents enjoy talking to customers and it shows.

According to the book, *The Top 100 Companies To Work For*, Southwest is in the top ten. They received the first ever Triple Crown Award from the Department of Transportation's air travel division. That means they ranked first in being on time, first in baggage handling, and first in customer satisfaction.

I've been on flights where the attendants sing the pre-flight routine and play games with the passengers such as the sock game. In the sock game, passengers take off their shoes and the person with the biggest hole in his sock wins an extra bag of peanuts.

On one flight, I recorded the flight attendant's pre-landing routine on my dictaphone. It was sung to the tune from the theme of the Beverly Hillbillies and had all of us in stitches.

The employees love their jobs. One flight attendant told me that her husband quit a job to go to work for Southwest for half as much, because of the culture that existed at Southwest.

And that's what it is — a culture. One where people love their work and consequently it spills over onto the customer. If people aren't treated as number one in their work then they can't treat the passenger as number one on the plane, on the phone and in the airport.

"There are two ways of exerting one's strength: one is pushing down, the other is pulling up." Push down on the employee and the customer is repressed as well. Elevate the employee and watch the employee put the customer on a pedestal.

"You can preach a better sermon with your life than with your lips."

— Oliver Goldsmith

• • •

The National Excellence in Leadership Association names four people throughout the United States to receive its annual award for outstanding leadership. Every ten years the association then names the top ten leaders for the decade from this list of forty people.

How prestigious is this award? Prior to the 1990s only one hundred fifty-eight awards had been presented. Only eleven recipients had been in the field of education. Lewis Mann is one of those eleven. He not only was one of the top ten leaders in that decade — he came in first place — he was named "the" leader of the decade in the United States.

I had the privilege of serving as master of ceremonies for the award presentation. My only qualification for the job was that Lewis Mann was my basketball coach for one year in high school. But like so many others — Lewis Mann had an impact on my life.

Lewis Mann became our basketball coach my junior year of high school. He recognized very quickly that our team suffered more from a lack of belief in ourselves than a lack of ability. He would know — he had coached at the junior college level where he had gained the reputation as a giant killer. He took a team of lesser talent and led them to a perfect record one year, capping the season with a four overtime win over the defending national champions.

That junior year of high school was particularly tough for me. I had injured my back but no doctor was able to diagnose the problem. I had to wear a back brace to participate in athletics — but still suffered a great deal of pain and I just couldn't move like I used to.

One day before practice Coach Mann brought a copy of *The Wichita Eagle* into our locker room. He had coerced a staff sports writer into writing an article on our little high school team. I realize now that it was for the sole purpose of building our self-esteem. The line that caught my eye was the one that quoted him as saying he had never had a player with as much courage as me — to play with that much pain when I couldn't even stand straight legged and bend over to pick a basketball off the floor. I've never forgotten that — it helped me at a time I needed it most.

Lewis Mann knew a lot about basketball but he knew more about people. He knew, "You can preach a better sermon with your life than with your lips." He was truly a role model. Lewis Mann may have made his reputation as a giant killer but it was he who stood as a giant.

"Few men are lacking in capacity, but they fail because they are lacking in application."

— Calvin Coolidge

• • •

The late Paul "Bear" Bryant, the winningest football coach in history, once said there are four kinds of players:

Those who have ability and know it.
Those who have ability and don't know it.
Those who don't have ability and know it.
Those who don't have ability and don't know it.

"The one that makes you proudest is the one who isn't good enough to play but it means so much to him, he puts so much into it that he does anyhow. We have lots of those. The ones who have ability and don't use it are the ones who eat your guts out."

I'll be the first to admit that people have different levels of potential and ability. The problem is that almost everyone, regardless of their level, fails to live up to that level. One of the reasons we don't is because we compare ourselves to other people. That is a dangerous trap.

There is an old adage in sports that you tend to play to the level of your competition. Good teams with good players can play poorly against teams with less ability. They still may win but nevertheless they only pushed themselves to that threshold of effort that allowed them to defeat the competition.

Eddie Sutton, coach of the Oklahoma State University men's basketball team, says that he is not so concerned with the team they are playing as he is about how his team will play. He figures that if his team plays to the best of their ability then they will win the games they should win.

Here's a way to gauge how close you are to reaching your full potential. Grade yourself on a scale of 1 to 10 in these critical areas of your life: Career, health, self-development, family, communication, organization and recreation. If you're like most people (and if you're honest with yourself) you'll discover you may be a little lopsided in some areas.

If Bear Bryant were to grade us, what category would he put us in? The Bear would probably say that most of us have a lot more ability than we are using.

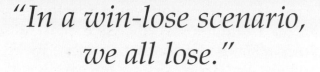

"In a win-lose scenario, we all lose."

— Brian Joiner

• • •

There's a lot of talk today about the win-win phi-losophy of interpersonal relationships. This makes sense because the only other alternatives are "win-lose" or "lose-lose." Somehow, there is a mistaken notion that if we come out on top in a win-lose relationship, whether it be with a customer, employee, employer, supplier or anyone else for that matter, that we do indeed "win." The results of this are devastating.

The best description of the outcome of a win-lose philosophy are in the words of psychologist Abraham Maslow. He said, "Everyone seems to be aware at some level of consciousness of the fact that authoritarian man-agement outrages the dignity of the worker. He then fights back in order to restore his dignity and self-esteem. He will do this actively, with hostility and vandalism and the like, or passively ... with all sorts of underhanded, sly and secretly vicious countermeasures. These reactions are puzzling generally to the denominator, but on the whole, they are easily enough understood, and they make very real psychological sense, if they are understood as attempts to maintain dignity under conditions of domi-nation or of disrespect."

Whenever we think we win at someone else's expense we are fooling ourselves. As Dr. Maslow so well states, when we take an authoritarian stance, the recipient reacts in kind — maybe not openly, but effectively just the same. We see this take place in athletics all the time. A coach robs a player of his self-esteem by publicly degrading him. The player responds with poorer performance or quits the team. Business is no different. We beat a supplier out of his last nickel on his price. He responds by cutting corners on quality or service. How else could they respond? Don't we react in the same way?

If we think "win-lose" is an acceptable outcome as long as we're the winner, then we have, in reality, accepted "lose-lose." The "loser" in the relationship retaliates. We get what we pay for — we reap what we sow.

Corporate America and our government are paying for the sins of generations of win-lose relations. Companies are suffering from losses today because of short term gain at the expense of customers and employees. Labor unions are losing members and power because of short term concessions at the expense of their members and the companies that employ them. The government is losing because of decades of reckless spending and mismanagement at the expense of the taxpayer.

The winners? There are none. Justice is truly blind. No one is exempt from the verdict of a win-lose philosophy. The losers lose and the winners do too. "In a win-lose scenario, we all lose."

"It is not for what we live, but for what we are prepared to die."

— Unknown

• • •

How passionate are you about what you're doing in life? Here's a pretty good test — are you prepared to die for what you believe? Sounds extreme doesn't it?

Get a group of World War II veterans together and you're bound to hear old war stories but if you listen closely you'll discover a deeper meaning in those tales.

When the Canadians entered World War II the elite fighting force of the Canadian armed services was called upon to engage in a dangerous mission. They were known as the Royal Rifles. The mission would be extremely dangerous they were told — so much so that it was considered suicidal. Odds were they wouldn't come back.

Forty-two hundred men were asked to put their lives on the line. They were given two day's leave immediately prior to embarking on their mission. Every man returned from leave — but only two-hundred returned from the mission. Four-thousand died.

Why would any soldier come back from two day's leave to participate in a suicide mission? At a reunion of the survivors many years later someone posed that question,"Why did you come back to face almost certain death?" The reason? "It is not for what we live, but for what we are prepared to die," was the reply.

Life is most precious when there is something for which we are prepared to die. The impact the lives of those four-thousand had on history is immeasurable. But the impact it had on the survivors may be the untold story. They had their lives in perspective when they accepted that mission. Life under a Nazi dictator would not be worth living, they must have reasoned, and death under the flag of freedom had meaning — if the purpose was to preserve that freedom.

One hundred Americans joined the Royal Rifles on that mission. They were the beginning of America's elite fighting force and distinguished themselves by adopting the headgear of the Royal Rifles. Many times since those dark days of World War II these Americans have been called upon to defend the Stars and Stripes, our symbol of freedom.

Who are they? They're best described in the lines of this song from the 1960s: "Men who mean just what they say, the brave men of the Green Beret." And what do they say? "It is not for what we live, but for what we are prepared to die."

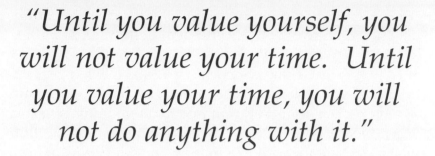

"Until you value yourself, you will not value your time. Until you value your time, you will not do anything with it."

— Dr. M. Scott Peck

• • •

I asked someone in one of my presentations to explain what time is. The respondent answered by saying that it was expensive. I had never heard time defined quite like that. It's true though — time is expensive. It can't be manufactured or saved.

Time's true value only becomes evident to us as we grow older and wistfully look back realizing that time slipped through our fingers and we can't quite understand how. The answer to this lies in the next few precious moments — even as you read this we take the time at hand for granted.

The question isn't, "How much time do we have?" We all have the same amount of time — twenty-four hours a day. The question is, "How do we squeeze the most value out of the time we have?"

Here's a good analogy of what time is worth. I learned this while consulting with Weaver Popcorn Company, Inc. Popcorn is popcorn, right? Not really. It all depends on how you use it that will determine its value.

If you buy bulk popcorn it costs about ten cents a pound. If you buy it in a fifty pound bag it will cost about sixteen cents a pound. Purchased in a two pound plastic bag popcorn sells for about twenty cents a pound. But when you sell popcorn in a microwave ready package its value goes up to $1.40 a pound! That's fourteen times the value of bulk popcorn! What's the difference? It's all popcorn — the difference is determined by how it's used.

Time is time, right? No. Just like popcorn its value is determined by how it's used. People who use their time properly gain the most value. Remember, time is expensive.

We measure our net worth in financial terms. Life is short — only when it is over will we be able to measure our true net worth. It will be measured by what we squeezed into our short lifetimes — what we did with the time that was allotted to us. That's a sobering thought isn't it? Your self-worth is determined largely by what you do with your time.

"Until you value yourself, you will not value your time." What are you worth? That's determined by how you use your time.

"Thou shalt not belly ache."

— David Ring

• • •

A CBS film crew rolls into Shidler, Oklahoma, a sleepy little town that barely appears on the state map. Why? To do a feature on "The One Armed Bandit." No, this isn't a story about a slot machine, but this one armed bandit pays off better than any in Las Vegas. "The One Armed Bandit" is the hottest specialty act on the Professional Rodeo Cowboys Association circuit and Las Vegas casinos haven't many acts that will top it.

John Payne is "The One Armed Bandit." He grew up in the hills of northern Oklahoma in the heart of cow country. And I know because John and I were close friends. He trained horses on his folk's ranch. I remember he once found a litter of baby raccoons and brought them home to raise. He had a pet hawk. John was a natural with animals.

When John was nineteen he lost his right arm in an electrical accident. Even though he was right handed he adapted, learned to use his left and continued his trade as a cowboy. He trained cowdogs and gained such a reputation that he was hired by ranches to gather cattle in places where no one else had been successful.

He eventually worked up his act which he presents in rodeos across the country. You have to see it to believe it. He has won the "Specialty Act of the Year Award" from the association every year since he was a rookie in 1989. No one before has even won it two years straight. He is known internationally.

John reminds me of a minister by the name of David Ring. He has cerebral palsy. All of his life he was told what he couldn't do — he couldn't play like other kids, he couldn't marry and have children and he couldn't go into the ministry.

He proved them all wrong. He married and has children. He preaches all over the country. He concludes his messages by saying, "I have cerebral palsy, what's your problem?" David Ring has an Eleventh Commandment, "Thou shalt not belly ache."

The message is clear, we all have problems. The question is not do we have problems, but are we using our problems as an excuse? David Ring and John Payne don't. "Thou shalt not belly ache." What's your problem?

" Thy actions, and thy actions alone, determine thy worth."

— Johann Fichte

• • •

When I was a youngster my Grandpa Whitt always carried a pocket watch that was commonly known in those days as a "dollar watch." The dollar watch received its name because it could be purchased at the local five and dime store for the measly sum of one dollar. The reason it was so cheap was that it was of such poor quality that it would stop working after only a short time.

Grandpa always had several discarded dollar watches lying around. One day he offered one to me as a gift. I know you're not supposed to look a gift horse in the mouth but I had to ask this question, "Does it run, Grandpa?" Grandpa just laughed and said, "Jim, it will run if you run."

Several years later it dawned on me what he meant. If I was carrying the watch in my pocket when I was running then the watch would be running with me.

All of us are carrying abilities and talents that we never use. The only thing we are lacking is action. In other words our ability and talent would run if we would run. If we don't, they lie dormant and therefore are useless. Why don't we act on these talents and abilities?

Many of us don't know what talents we really possess. If we would try something we've never done before we might discover that we're good at it. Sometimes we're fearful of failure. If we fail, so what? We've at least given it a shot. Sometimes we're just too complacent. Trying something challenging and new requires effort. Maybe we're too comfortable or just too lazy.

There really isn't that much difference between high achievers and the rest of the population. One difference is that they take action. When most people are wondering what they could do, others are out doing it.

Taking action is the result of making a decision to do so. A friend of mine recently made this statement, "Once you decide what you're going to do it's amazing the things that happen."

"Thy actions, and thy actions alone, determine thy worth." Just like Grandpa's dollar watch, your abilities and talents will run when you run.

"Action without vision just passes the time."

— Joel Barker

• • •

As a consultant and speaker I stress the importance of vision and goals and consider them to be of paramount importance. There is a problem in achieving our vision and our goals, however. First, if our goals don't make our pulse quicken when we think or talk about them then our problem is simple — they aren't big enough.

I was consulting with a business that is based in Texas and has branches throughout the southeastern United States. During our planning conference with the staff I asked everyone to tell me where they thought the business could be in ten years. The company's president stated that he could see them as an international corporation in ten years. You could see the eyes light up in the room — people got excited and it's no wonder, the goal suddenly became exciting.

The second problem is this, even if our vision and goals are big enough they won't happen just because we want them to. Ask yourself this question, "What am I doing right now to push myself closer to my goals? Not tomorrow, not next week but right now, today?" The ability to single mindedly focus our attention on one goal is one of the most important attributes of successful people. Are your goals lost in the shuffle of the mundane tasks that could be and should be delegated to others? Why do the giants of business become giants? They focus on what they do best and delegate the rest.

Every day ask yourself, "What am I doing? Is it important? Can someone else do it?" If not, then STOP! FOCUS on your goals — write them down, overhaul them, rewrite them — then do whatever it takes to get you there. Don't waste your time on things that really aren't important.

Is it important? Then as Bo Jackson said — JUST DO IT!

"Nothing will ever be attempted if all possible objections must first be overcome."

— Unknown

• • •

How did Japan become a world leader in technology and manufacturing in less than half a century after they were defeated in World War II? A good portion of Japan was leveled after two atomic bombs. They couldn't make excuses for why something wouldn't work — they had nothing to work with. They committed themselves to long range goals and quality. It worked!

Time after time we've seen people who have come from backgrounds of poverty or extreme adversity go on to become tremendously successful. We applaud their efforts and wonder how they achieved so much with so little. That's the advantage truly disadvantaged people have — they don't have anything to lose so they go for broke and in the process they succeed.

In either case — be it an individual or a country — tremendous adversity was overcome to achieve excellence. So why do the disadvantaged overachieve while the advantaged tend to underachieve? I believe it's because we attain a certain level of success and then become fearful of risking what we have to attain more.

Someone once told me that we spend half of our life worrying about how we're going to make anything and the other half worrying about how to keep from losing it. He's right — we become fearful of losing our moderate standard of success in pursuit of more.

Have you ever said something like this: "Someday I'll...." Guess what, SOMEDAY NEVER COMES! People, organizations and yes, even countries achieve greatness because they seize the moment, they act now and they don't make excuses for why they can't.

Benjamin Disraeli observed, "Life's too short to be little." Our lives are short and yet we wait and wait and wait.

"Nothing will ever be attempted if all possible objections must first be overcome." What are you waiting for? I know — someday I'll ...

"I was not the lion, but it fell to me to give the lion's roar."

— Winston Churchill

• • •

Leadership is a much talked about virtue in business today. We may think we know what leadership is but when asked to define it we are usually at a loss for words. One way to define leadership is to examine the traits of great leaders.

Winston Churchill provided hope to Britain and the rest of the free world during World War II. He was unwavering in his belief and articulated this belief through his speeches and radio broadcasts. He defined who the British people were, what they stood for and where they were going. As he said, " I was not the lion, but it fell to me to give the lion's roar." Without his leadership the outcome of World War II might have been much different. He had credibility and a strong philosophy.

Charles O'Reilly of the University of California, Berkeley, investigated the credibility of the top management of three companies. The conclusion from this study was that when top management is perceived to have high credibility and a strong philosophy, employees are more likely to :

(1) Be proud to tell others they are part of the organization.

(2) Talk up the organization with friends.
(3) See their own values as similar to those of the organization.
(4) Feel a sense of ownership for the organization.

When management is perceived to have low credibility, employees are more likely to believe that other company employees:

(1) Produce only when watched.
(2) Are motivated primarily by money.
(3) Say good things about the organization at work, but feel differently in private.
(4) Would consider looking for another job if the organization were experiencing tough times.

Great leaders have a strongly held philosophy and "sell" that philosophy to others in the organization in the form of a mission statement. It includes the purpose, vision and values. When this is effectively communicated then others "buy" it. This gives a sense of ownership. It enables others to align their values with the values of the leadership.

All leaders, whether it be in a company, an association or as a parent at home, can build credibility by developing a strongly held philosophy and sharing that philosophy. Like Winston Churchill, you may not be the lion but it falls on you to give the lion's roar.

"If I can make people laugh, then I have served my purpose for God."

— Red Skelton

• • •

Our family always enjoyed the comic strip *Calvin and Hobbes*. In one strip, Calvin runs up to his friend and asks,"Suzie, do you want to trade Captain Napalm bubble gum cards? After chewing almost twenty dollars worth of gum, I've collected all the cards except numbers eight and thirty-four. I'll trade you any duplicate for either of those." In the next frame Suzie responds,"I don't collect Captain Napalm bubble cards." Calvin dejectedly walks away saying,"It must be depressing to go through life with no purpose."

We can laugh about Calvin's purpose of "collecting Captain Napalm bubble gum cards," but he's right — it is depressing to go through life with no purpose. That's why people become suicidal — it's not because they want to die — they simply see no purpose in living.

Everyone has a purpose in life. Very few people ever come to that realization but those who discover their purpose and act on it are destined to fulfill their unique potential. Even a comedian has a purpose, for as Red Skelton said,"If I can make people laugh, then I have served my purpose for God."

Comedian Argus Hamilton has been called the "Will Rogers of today" by fellow comedian Robin Williams. Hamilton is from Oklahoma so the comparison is inevitable. Argus Hamilton is a black sheep of sorts though. His father and grandfather were Methodist ministers. In fact, his grandfather married my parents back in 1942. If we look a little deeper, however, we might discover that he may not be a black sheep after all. An article I read revealed he has a purposeful perspective of life:

"I try to remember that I'm just in the efforts business, God is in the results business. If I can stay in the efforts and out of the results — results take care of themselves. After years and years, I've learned that God has better plans for me than I do. As long as I put one foot in front of the other and keep going toward this goal, something miraculous will probably happen that I hadn't even planned on. For people who are motivated, God answers prayer in one of three ways: 'Yes,' 'Not yet,' or 'I've got something better for you.' "

Argus Hamilton didn't set out to be a comedian — he studied law in college. But that simply wasn't the right vehicle to fulfill his purpose in life. I guess God knew the last thing we needed was another lawyer — but that we could always stand a little more laughter. That's why Argus Hamilton, like Red Skelton, can say,"If I can make people laugh, then I have served my purpose for God."

"Self trust is the first secret of success."

— Ralph Waldo Emerson

• • •

You remember Victor Kiam as "the man who bought the company" when he advertised Remington electric razors on television. In the August 2, 1988 edition of *USA Today*, Kiam was quoted as saying, "To be a successful entrepreneur, you must not be afraid to bet on yourself."

Why are we afraid to bet on ourselves as Victor Kiam puts it? If Emerson is right and self trust is the first secret of success then we just need to trust ourselves.

Here's a simple formula for building that self trust. There is much research that supports the theory that the mind cannot distinguish the difference between a real or an imagined experience. We store information in our minds in the form of pictures.

To prove this point think of a memorable moment in your life, one that was a milestone perhaps, when you scored a touchdown or maybe performed well in a piano recital. Replay this past success on your mental motion picture screen. Experience the emotions, the feelings, the sights, sounds and smells. It's very vivid, isn't it?

Now think about something you want to try that

may push you out of your comfort zone — something you've wanted to attempt but maybe said, "I could never do that." But first pull up that past success on your mental motion picture screen — replay it again and again. You'll feel your confidence grow with each replay. Recapture those same feelings and sensations.

Now substitute the thing you want to attempt on your mental screen. The successful feelings are there, the emotion is there — the same mental frame of mind will allow you to see yourself succeeding at the new task or goal. If you can see yourself succeeding in your mind's eye then you can succeed in real life — because the mind cannot distinguish between a real and an imagined experience. You've just got to trust yourself to do it for real.

"Self trust is the first secret of success." "It works — trust me. Or better yet — trust yourself."

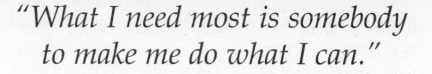

"What I need most is somebody to make me do what I can."

— Ralph Waldo Emerson

• • •

My friend Monty Teeter once asked me how I would describe my work as a consultant, writer and professional speaker. I fumbled around trying to articulate a reasonable definition. Finally, he said that what I really was is a "professional provoker." That was a good definition. I provoke people to challenge what they do, why they do it and how to change it.

All of us settle into what we call ruts. This is also known as our comfort zone. It requires absolutely no effort to slide into our rut but it certainly takes effort to rise out of it. Sometimes it's more a matter of not being aware that we are in a rut. Awareness is the first step out of our comfort zone and this realization may come in many shapes and forms.

Enter the professional provoker. Perhaps we read something or hear a speaker who provokes us to take stock of ourselves and get with the program. More often though, the provoker comes disguised as failure, adversity or hardship. An unfortunate fact of human nature is that sometimes we must be driven to our knees before we have sense enough to challenge the status quo.

I remember reading Lee Iacocca's autobiography a few years ago. Before he gained fame selling cars on television as Chrysler's Chairman, he was President of Ford — until he was fired. Then he took over at Chrysler.

His ego was probably shattered, but that firing was the best incentive he could have to get the moribund Chrysler Corporation back on its feet and running. He was provoked. Odds are most of us wouldn't have even known who Lee Iacocca was if he had stayed on at Ford. He got out of his comfort zone but it took losing his job to do it.

The best provoker we can have is ourselves, however. Why wait for tragedy to strike? We should be proactive rather than reactive.

"What I need most is somebody to make me do what I can." That somebody stares at me in the mirror every morning. The question is, "Will I make myself do what I can?"

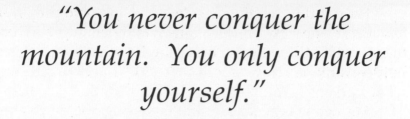

"You never conquer the mountain. You only conquer yourself."

— Jim Whittaker, the first American to climb Mt. Everest

• • •

I had to discipline one of my children for an act of disobedience. I explained he was being his own worst enemy. It dawned on me a little later that the same could be said about me — I am my own worst enemy. If we conquer ourselves, we conquer our problems. How can we accomplish this?

First, accept responsibility for our own actions and quit blaming circumstances, other people, the weather, etc. Life is a series of choices — our choices. The employees blame the boss, the boss blames the employees, both blame the customer — where does it stop? As Harry Truman said, "The buck stops here."

Second, do battle with ourselves — if we are to conquer, we must go to war. Get tough with ourselves. If we only read one self-help book a month we would be in the upper one per cent of the population in self-development. Imagine that — what a small price to pay to win the war with ourselves. Olympic athletes train for hours a day for weeks, months and years to prepare for only an opportunity to compete for a gold medal. We tend to think success will just happen.

Finally, quit talking a good game and start playing. Have you ever noticed how easy it is to tell others what they need to do, yet we won't practice what we preach? As a consultant, I think about that a lot — am I practicing what I preach? You've got to "walk the talk."

If you're like me, life seems to be full of problems sometimes. They're like mountains — not just one but a whole range. They're big — how will I conquer them? By conquering only one, the tallest one — then the road will all be downhill. The tallest mountain is, of course, myself.

Let's put on our hiking boots — and conquer ourselves.

"Nothing in the world can take the place of persistence. Talent will not... Genius will not... Education will not... Persistence, and persistence alone, always has, and always will, solve the problems of the human race."

— Calvin Coolidge

• • •

You get the feeling that silent Cal felt pretty strongly about the subject of persistence. Known more as a man of will than of words this creed served him well as President of the United States.

Everyone wants to quit sometimes. I like what Charles "Tremendous" Jones has to say about the subject: "Just because you want to quit, doesn't mean you have to quit." We all live a life of peaks and valleys — it's when we're in the valley we have to be on guard. It takes no persistence at all when we're on the mountain top. What we have to remember is that it took persistence to get there.

Successful people in every walk of life have become

so through persistence. We've all heard of the many failures of the great figures of history. Thomas Edison performed over 10,000 unsuccessful experiments before perfecting the light bulb. Abraham Lincoln ran for office unsuccessfully ten times before being elected President. Winston Churchill was ridiculed as a radical before becoming Prime Minister at a time when Britain and the world needed someone with his persistence.

Churchill is one of my favorites. In my opinion, he is the man who made the most impact on the Twentieth Century. He warned England and the rest of the world for years about Adolf Hitler and no one listened — yet he persisted — and fortunately for us he did.

I've used the following illustration many times in speeches and seminars. When asked to address a commencement exercise after the war, Churchill rose to his feet, leaned forward on his cane, and with the famous bulldog expression upon his face uttered these words, "Never give up. Never, never give up." With that he sat down. Only seven words — is there any doubt about what made him great?

Persistence.

"I care not so much what I am in the opinion of others as what I am in my own."

— Michel de Montaigne

• • •

Barbara Reynolds wrote an article that appeared in the February 14, 1992 issue of *USA Today* entitled *Haley Rose From the Depths to Take Us All to New Heights*. The article was about the late Alex Haley who became famous for his novel *Roots* that ultimately became a TV miniseries.

Reynolds told of how Haley nearly gave up on his novel before it was complete. In his words, "A lot of black scholars told me not to write *Roots*. They said it would never amount to anything because it was about slavery. Almost everybody I knew was against the book. I was tired, beaten down. It looked like I was hanging on to something worthless."

This rejection by his peers nearly drove Haley to suicide according to Reynolds. Of course, Haley did complete the novel and it became a classic during his own lifetime.

What a fine thread that holds our futures. Had Alex Haley listened to his critics who were cleverly disguised as friends, *Roots* would never have become a reality and he may have taken his own life.

What impact did this have on Barbara Reynolds? "Haley's experience persuaded me to purge myself of negative thinking friends."

I like Ms. Reynolds choice of words: "To purge myself of negative thinking friends." One definition of purge is, "To cleanse of impurities or foreign matter." Negative people are foreign matter. They attack our minds like bacteria attacks our bodies — breaking down our immune system until we can no longer resist the disease that results.

We expect to be discouraged by our enemies — we may not like it but we can accept it. It's painful to experience discouragement from our friends, however. Regardless, we cannot afford the luxury of their company if it is detrimental. Like we tell our children, you become like the company you keep.

"I care not so much what I am in the opinion of others as what I am in my own." Your opinion will be much higher if you purge yourself of your negative thinking "friends."

"Sow a thought, reap an action; sow an action, reap a habit; sow a habit, reap a character; sow a character, reap a destiny."

— Ralph Waldo Emerson

• • •

Mel Winger, a friend who owns a large farming operation, and I were visiting on the phone one day about how we never can get enough training in the area of people skills. He made a good analogy, "It's like planting corn — you have to stop periodically and fill your planter with seed." I like that — a lot of us are out sowing with an empty planter. When harvest rolls around there's not much to reap and we scratch our heads and wonder why — our planter ran out of seed and we didn't fill it up.

When I visit with prospective clients I can tell pretty fast whether they can use my services. One dead give-away is if they reply, "I think we're already doing a good job. I don't really see any need to train our people." You can bet the farm they need the training more than anyone else. Their planter ran out of seed a long time ago and they never bothered to fill it up. Their harvest is going to be pretty slim.

In Steven Covey's book, *The 7 Habits of Highly Effective People*, a main theme is this — for us to more effectively deal with people, we have to be better people ourselves. Here's a passage I think sums it up, "It's a painful process. It's a change that has to be motivated by a higher purpose, but the willingness to subordinate what you think you want now for what you want later. But this process produces happiness, 'the object and design of our existence.' Happiness can be defined, in part at least, as the fruit of the desire and ability to sacrifice what we want now for what we want eventually."

During corn planting time we wouldn't dream of neglecting to fill the planter with seed because we just didn't have the time — and yet we neglect to fill our minds with seed because we just don't have the time. This is immediately followed by much complaining about the harvest — in our relationships with our customers, our associates, our boss, our co-workers or our family.

We need to ask ourselves if we haven't invested a lot of money and time in land, machinery, preparation and fertilizer only to forget to put seed in our planters. What will we harvest?

"For whatsoever a man soweth, that shall he also reap."

"Obstacles will look large or small to you according to whether you are large or small."

— Orison Swett Marden

• • •

Glenn Rehbein of Lino Lakes, Minnesota built a business from scratch back in the 1950s to one that does millions in sales every year today. Glenn and I were visiting one day about how business can be so good that it actually creates a problem — there doesn't seem to be enough hours in the day to accomplish all we need to do. Glenn shared this philosophy with me. He said that there are three problems that you'll always face in business — you'll be short of help, short of work or short of money.

That's really true, we'll never be free of problems in business or life. Even when business is good, that in itself creates problems. But those are the right kind of problems to have. We'll never be without problems and that's good — without problems there is no reason for our existence. A successful business is one that solves problems through the sale of a product or service. A successful person is one who solves problems.

Years ago I had the privilege of hearing Dr. Norman Vincent Peale speak at a convention in St. Louis. His speech was entitled "Power Over Problems." He related a story about a friend who wanted advice on how to eliminate all of his problems. Dr. Peale stated that he could take him to a place where the residents had absolutely no problems whatever. The friend was encouraged until Dr. Peale told him the place was a cemetery in the Bronx.

In other words the only people without problems are dead! He therefore concluded that it was logical to assume that the more problems we have the more alive we are. If we buy into that then we must accept the fact that the higher we go in life the more problems we will experience.

Dwight D. Eisenhower told John F. Kennedy the day before Kennedy was inaugurated that, "You'll find that no easy problems ever come to the President of the United States. If they are easy to solve, then somebody else has solved them." The lesson here is that if you aspire to be successful then you must be willing to deal with more and bigger problems.

"Obstacles will look large or small to you according to whether you are large or small." Are you experiencing more and bigger problems? Great! That means you are becoming a bigger person. But as you grow your problems will look smaller.

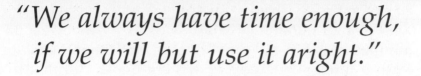

"We always have time enough, if we will but use it aright."

— Johann Wolfgang von Goethe

• • •

"I don't have time." Come on — let's be honest — when we say we don't have time we really don't mean it. The truth of the matter is that we do have time. We are all truly equal in that respect — we all have twenty-four hours a day. What we really should say is this, "I'd rather spend my time doing something else" or "That is not a priority for me — I've committed my time to something else."

"I don't have time" is the greatest excuse for "I don't want to." It's a choice — we choose to spend our time the way we want to. "But I've got work to do," you might say. That work is your choice — you choose your vocation — no one does that for you.

Have you ever noticed that we always find the time to do the things we want to do? Sure we do. Let me share a way to "make" more time. You've got twenty-four hours or 1,440 minutes a day. Could you spare one percent of your time to work on something worthwhile each day? That's 14.4 minutes. Let's be generous and round up to 15 minutes a day.

What can you do with 15 minutes? You can become

an expert on any subject you care to study in three years with just 15 minutes of study a day. By investing 15 minutes a day for one year you could read the entire Bible, learn a foreign language or write a book. All that by investing only one per cent of your time. How's that for a return on your investment?

One of the best investments of my time has been reading and listening to positive, motivational material. Let's look at our analogy of the one percent investment again. If I invest only one percent of my time in an imaginary savings account for self-development then I have 87.6 hours of positive thoughts that I can withdraw after only one year! If you're like me I need this to pay on the accumulated debt of negative thoughts that I find in my mental mail box every day. Come to think of it, maybe I need to increase my investment.

Let's open an account — the bills are piling up.

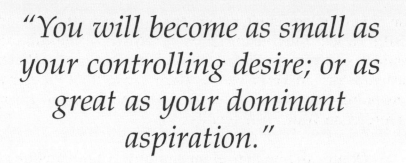

"You will become as small as your controlling desire; or as great as your dominant aspiration."

— James Allen

• • •

We've all been to the circus to see the elephants perform. It's always amazing to me how one or two average size human beings can direct the activities of a small herd of elephants that weigh several tons each. Did you ever wonder what keeps those elephants from running away? How can they be controlled?

Shortly after birth the baby elephants are tied to a tree with a piece of rope. At this tender age their strength is not overpowering. They struggle against the rope until they realize that it's a lost cause. Once they've been conditioned to believe the rope will control them they never try to break free again.

As full grown pachyderms they are tethered to a stake. They can pull up the stake or break the rope anytime they wish but as far as they're concerned they are bound just as firmly to that stake as an adult as they were to the tree in their infancy.

Psychologists refer to this phenomenon as "learned helplessness." Perception is a powerful force. Perception is stronger than reality — in fact perception is reality. There is research that supports the theory that the mind cannot differentiate between a real and an imagined experience.

Control is a matter of perception. There are things over which we have control that we think we don't. Often times we think we are controlled by people or circumstances. In a free society, such as we enjoy, other people only control us if we give them our permission.

You may counter by saying that your "boss" controls you because of your job. Not really — you have elected to work for that boss — you may elect to change jobs.

You may believe that your spouse controls you. As an adult you may believe your mother or father controls you. Yet none of them holds any power over you — you can choose to lead your life as you please.

The issue is, "Who's in control of your life?" Are you tied to a tree or merely tethered to a stake with the ability to break free any time you wish. "You will become as small as your controlling desire; or as great as your dominant aspiration."

"Only begin and then the mind grows heated. Only begin and the task will be completed."

— Goethe

• • •

As April 15 nears, millions of people across the United States anguish over the thought of income tax — myself included. We know it has to be done but we put it off and then fret about it. Will it get any easier if we wait? Of course not — in fact the opposite is true. Once we get into it, we get it out of the way and regardless of the outcome we heave a sigh of relief.

Successful people don't procrastinate. Instead of thinking about doing something, they do it. I'm fully convinced that this is one of the common denominators of all successful people. High achievers in any field dive into something, mess it up, overhaul it, repackage it and before you know it they have accomplished a seemingly impossible task.

People ask me how I come up with ideas for what I write. I'm almost ashamed to tell them. I sit down at my computer or with a pen and paper and start writing. I reread it, make some changes and it's almost difficult to stop. Once our creativity is kicked into gear it goes into overdrive. I never wrote poetry in my life but I have written poems to use in speeches since I started speaking professionally. I didn't know I could do that — it just happened when I started.

Experience has taught me that 90% of completing a project is beginning. You might say that you know lots of people who start things and never finish. But have you ever known anyone who finished something they didn't start?

We all know of things that we need or want to do but because we can't see the light at the end of the tunnel we don't start. Elegant solutions rarely present themselves at first. Once we begin, rough solutions become refined.

Let's get started.

"An adventure is the deliberate, volitional movement out of the comfort zone."

— James W. Newman

• • •

Picture yourself sitting in front of the television set, watching your favorite sitcom or soap. The announcer breaks in to proclaim, "We've run out of shows! You'll just have to go out and live your lives instead of sitting there watching us!" This is what happened to Garfield, the fat, lazy, lovable couch potato cat in a comic strip. The announcer continues, "Just kidding!" Garfield breathes a sigh of relief.

Television can become a substitute for living. Instead of living our lives we can simply pop some popcorn and live our lives through characters on a TV program.

Someone discovered that at the young age of forty she had terminal cancer. The doctor gave her only a year to live. Upon learning this she said, "I need to make a list! There is so much I want to do!" What would we do if we discovered we only had one year to live? We'd get up off the couch, kick a hole in the TV, make a list and do those things that we always said we'd do "someday." Well, someday is here. It always has been because we don't know whether or not we have one year to live.

A survey of college graduates revealed they would prefer to work for a large company rather than go into business themselves. The reason was to avoid the "R" word — that word which has become obscene in the American vocabulary — RISK! Why do we avoid risk? Fear of failure! So what? If we only had one year to live, would we care? Of course not.

To get out of our comfort zones we must focus on the "A" word — ADVENTURE! That's right. Instead of looking at the risk, look at the adventure. Several years ago, a couple of friends and I went to Panama to prospect for gold. We came home a few thousand dollars poorer and a lot wiser. For a long time I kicked myself for pulling such a stupid stunt. I took a risk and failed.

Today I can look back on that experience for what it really was — an adventure. I haven't run into many people who have prospected for gold in Panama and as a professional speaker it makes a great story to tell — crowds love it. In fact that adventure, though expensive at the time, has paid me back many times in speaker's fees.

"An adventure is the deliberate, volitional movement out of the comfort zone." Life's too short to be comfortable — let's live — while there's still time.

"The source and center of all man's creative power ... is his power of making images, or the power of imagination."

— Robert Collier

• • •

We've all heard the phrase "paint the town" but should you venture through Hominy, Oklahoma, you'll discover someone really did "paint the town." That someone is Cha´ Tullis, an artist who brings his Indian heritage to life through murals painted on the sides of businesses throughout the community. People travel from all over just to see the "visions" that Cha´ has reproduced in larger than life, living color. Visions? That's right, visions.

I had the opportunity to visit with Cha´ about how he creates his murals. The scenes depict Indian lore — there's a meaning or a message, not just a picture. Cha´ describes his artistic ability as a gift. He didn't always use his gift — until he decided to follow his dream. He wanted to study art after high school but was encouraged by his father to do something more practical — so Cha' got into the jewelry business. He was very successful. He owned two stores and acquired a very comfortable lifestyle. But something was lacking — the "gift." And what was the gift? The ability to convert "visions" into art.

Cha´ started using this gift. He would have these "visions" at night while he slept. He kept a pad next to his bed and upon awakening from the vision he would sketch as much as possible and note the colors he saw in his dream. The murals that you see around Hominy are the tangible re-creation of his visions.

I asked Cha´ how he would advise a young person who was given the choice to do something "practical" or "follow his dream." He answered without hesitation, "Follow the dream. Follow the dream until you die." I asked why. "Because it's a form of death if you don't," was his answer.

Like Cha´ Tullis we are given the power to dream, imagine and visualize. And like Cha´, sometimes our dreams are killed — by a well-meaning desire to be "practical." And when our dream is killed we follow it to the grave — "a form of death." But it's not too late. Like Cha´ Tullis, we can be resurrected from this form of death when we decide to follow our dream. Cha´ Tullis realized his visions and the power to convert them into art were a gift — one that he had to use or lose.

"The source and center of all man's creative power ... is his power of making images, or the power of imagination." All of us have a gift. All of us have a dream. All of us have the power to convert that dream into reality. Cha´ Tullis decided to use his gift — that was the day the world lost a jeweler and gained an artist — and Cha´ Tullis started to live.

"There's no traffic jam on the extra mile."

— Anonymous

• • •

While living on the farm we had a rural mail carrier to be a different sort — he went against the grain of the rural work ethic. Sometimes a package was too big for our mailbox. Instead of delivering the package to our house which was 150 yards off the county road, he sat and honked. If we walked down the drive to get our package, fine — if we didn't, he left a notice and drove on.

I complained to our local postmaster. She explained she was helpless to do anything because the carrier's union contract required him to only deliver to the box — not to the house and certainly not to get out of his vehicle. Unlike most mail carriers, he did only what was required, nothing more. You can imagine how popular he was on our route.

On the other hand our UPS man was different — his name was Joe. He made a point to call me by my first name, gave excellent service and always visited for a minute or two when he delivered a package. I liked Joe. He did more than his job required — he added a personal touch. In fact, I always looked forward to receiving a package by UPS because it meant a visit with Joe.

When people sent me packages, I requested they

send them UPS. Apparently our rural mail carrier never discovered that I had a choice.

The best way to insure job security is to do more than we are required. We don't have to, but somewhere out there is a competitor who may be just a little bit hungrier than we are. Maybe he doesn't have a union contract or a job description that tells him he doesn't have to just put in his time and go home.

Maybe he really cares about his customers and wants to please them. Scary isn't it?

Let's go the extra mile — we can make good time because there's not much traffic.

"Always try to see life around you as if you'd just come out of a tunnel."

— From the movie Mr. Smith Goes to Washington

• • •

I am truly thankful for the classic films from the golden age of Hollywood. Good triumphs over evil in these old movies and we're treated to a moral along the way. One of my favorites is *Mr. Smith Goes to Washington*. Jimmy Stewart plays the role of the idealistic, young Senator Jefferson Smith who goes to Washington only to find it filled with graft and corruption.

In one scene, Senator Smith visits with his secretary about life back in his home state and the virtues passed on to him by his father. "Have you ever noticed how grateful you are to see daylight after coming through a long dark tunnel? Always try to see life around you as if you'd just come out of a tunnel," was a philosophy his father had shared with him as a boy.

That's good advice. The movie was made in the 1930s. Mr. Smith would find Washington much in the same shape today — maybe even worse. There always has been and always will be things in life that disgust us and we wonder if life really is worth it.

It's all a matter of perception. If we focus on the bad we become paranoid. We think that there is a conspiracy to inhibit our success. We've all heard of Murphy's Law, "Whatever can go wrong will." Then there are those who are really paranoid that insist that Murphy was an optimist!

On the other hand we can adopt the attitude of W. Clement Stone, a self-proclaimed inverse paranoid. What's an inverse paranoid? That's someone who believes that there's a conspiracy afoot to guarantee success! It must work. Mr. Stone built the Combined Insurance Companies of America which has six billion dollars in assets using that philosophy.

"Every day is a good day," says Zig Ziglar. "If you don't believe it just try missing one!" Are you alive? Then focus on the good. What you see is what you get. If you focus on the tunnel you'll only see darkness. Focus on the light at the end of the tunnel. Take a deep breath, smell the flowers, hear the birds sing and bathe in the warmth of the brilliant sunlight of a summer's day.

"Always try to see life as if you'd just come out of a tunnel." Live life to the fullest. Each day is a gift. We should tear the wrapping paper off each day like a kid at Christmas. If we do, we'll appreciate life a lot more.

"I will pay more for the ability to get along with other people than any other skill."

— Charles Schwab

• • •

When Tony Angelino was a youngster his father had a vending machine business. When Tony was old enough he went to work for his dad. Tony was good at repairing the machines when they malfunctioned but encountered problems in dealing with customers. As Tony put it, "Whenever customers called about a machine that needed repairing, they were already mad when you arrived."

Tony's father asked him how he was getting along in his new job. Tony explained that he had no problem with fixing the machines but he was weary of dealing with irate customers. His father laughed and told him that anyone could fix a machine but not everyone could fix the customer.

We deal with two kinds of customers. The external customer — those who purchase our product and service and the internal customer — those with whom we deal inside our organizations in the process of serving the external customer.

People skills are becoming increasingly important in our jobs. In one of my seminars a supervisor insightfully observed, "When I first started out with this company your performance was measured by how high you could throw a hundred pound bag." His comment was well taken. He was enrolled in the seminar to develop his supervisory skills and found it difficult. Another participant stated that he didn't buy into all this diplomacy in dealing with people. But times change and so must we if we are to survive.

People skills are just that — skills. Maybe the problem is that we view people skills as diplomacy or manipulation or being nice. The fact is they are skills that are essential to our success. Being diplomatic or nice has nothing to do with it.

No one would question the value of learning a technical skill to be proficient in our work. In fact, we wouldn't dream of filling a position with someone who wasn't technically competent. Why should we view skills in dealing with people any differently? Like technical skills, people skills can be learned.

Charles Schwab said that he would pay more for the ability to get along with other people than any other skill. Remember, anyone can fix a machine but not everyone can fix a customer. Those who develop people skills can effectively deal with internal and external customers and those skills will earn them more than any other.

"Keep away from people who try to belittle your ambitions. Small people always do that, but the really great make you feel that you, too, can become great."

— Mark Twain

• • •

I have a philosophy that I strictly adhere to — stay away from negative people. This is difficult to do, I admit. It's nearly impossible because negative people sometimes include family or friends.

Have you ever noticed it seems some people's mission in life is to take you down a notch or two? That's because they feel inferior to you. The only way they can build themselves up is by tearing you down. They can't see themselves accomplishing anything great so they don't want you to either.

The flip side of this is to seek out and build relationships with positive people. Why? Positive people see themselves as high achievers. They aren't threatened by the success of others so they help others become high achievers too.

Truly successful people want you to be a success too. They'll share whatever time and resources they have to help you accomplish your goals. Not only that, they'll listen to what you have to say because they feel like they can learn something from you as well.

Think of it like this — negative people drain your battery. Positive people are like a generator — they recharge your battery. You can be down (discharged) and a visit with one of your positive associates is like a jump start — it gets you started until you can recharge your own battery.

We need to ask ourselves if we're positive or negative people. Do people walk away charged up or drained after a visit with us? Do we encourage others and dare them to be great? This might be the difference in their lives. Someone along the way surely spoke an encouraging word to the Lincolns, Edisons and Einsteins of this world. At times a word of encouragement means so much.

Associate with great people — you'll become great in the process.

"Why not go out on a limb? Isn't that where the fruit is?"

— Frank Scully

• • •

We all want to go to heaven but we don't want to die to get there. Success and failure are the same way — we all want to succeed but we don't want to fail in the process. This fear of failure has probably done more to keep people from reaching their full potential than anything else.

We all want to taste the fruit of success. The rub is this — we don't want to crawl out on that limb. We'll scoot out there a little bit and look down — it looks like a million miles to the ground! We'll crawl out a little farther — the limb bends earthward — will it break? Our pulse quickens and our palms sweat. Maybe we ought to turn back.

This isn't easy either — you can't turn around — you have to crawl backwards. It's decision making time — do we go for it? Or do we shinny back down the tree and wait for the fruit to fall in our laps?

If you're like me the preceding paragraph seemed all too real and familiar as I wrote it. But how do we convince ourselves that the fruit is worth the risk of going out on a limb?

Failure and success are directly proportional — in other words, risk a little, enjoy a little success. Risk much, enjoy much success. If you want to enjoy the highest degree of success, then you must be willing to risk the highest degree of failure. That's right, you must be willing to fail — and fail miserably. Sounds tough doesn't it?

When entertaining a risky venture, ask yourself, "What's the worst thing that can happen?" Then, "Can I accept that?" You can? Great! Go for it. I've used this method several times over the years. Each time of crisis builds faith and confidence. Yes I have failed — but I've won a few, too. You see, you really fail your way to success. Every failure increases your odds of succeeding — you've simply eliminated another way to fail.

It often takes something traumatic to put failure in perspective. My wife called one day when I was away on a business trip. She told me she had been involved in an automobile accident. Fortunately, she was not injured. It makes you think — cars, like all material things can be replaced — people can't.

By comparison what do we really have to lose? I can accept that.

"Coaches who can outline plays on a blackboard are a dime a dozen. The ones who win can get inside their players and motivate."

— Vince Lombardi

• • •

As coach of the Green Bay Packers, Vince Lombardi led his team to six divisional titles, five National Championships and the first two Super Bowls during the 1960s. I'm sure that he would have been the first to admit that other coaches may have known more about the game of football. He was head and shoulders above most others in one respect however, he knew how to mold a group of people into a team with a common purpose. He was the consummate motivator.

Motivation is almost a dirty word in some circles today. I listened to a cassette recording recently that referred to motivation as the "M" word — one to avoid using.

Why? Maybe it's because we think that people who are excited about what they're doing and preach the motivational gospel are just too unsophisticated. It's a good thing someone forgot to tell Sam Walton that or he might not have motivated his employees into making Wal-Mart Stores, Inc. the number one retail business in the world.

Motivation is simply providing a motive that incites people to action. Studies show that what people want most out of their work is meaning and recognition. Those are motives that don't cost anything and successful leaders supply them.

H. Ross Perot, self-made billionaire gained a lot of attention as an independent candidate for President of the United States in 1992. Perot had this to say concerning motivating people in the work place: "Is it better for you to make me enjoy my work or hate my work? The answer is simple. Yet all over corporate America, we've got guys who show up every morning and make people just as miserable as they can."

Effective motivators aren't all fluff and no substance. In fact they are usually tough, hard nosed realists with high expectations for themselves and others. No one ever accused Lombardi, Walton or Perot as being pushovers.

"Coaches who can outline plays on a blackboard are a dime a dozen. The ones who win get inside their players and motivate." Successful leaders provide people with a motive that incites them to action. Successful leaders are enthusiastic, they encourage and empower others — they get inside their people and motivate.

"If you would be remembered, do one thing superbly well."

— Saunders Norvell

• • •

I was driving a straight stretch of highway one day — it was a beautiful summer morning. A couple of miles up ahead, I could see a crop duster spraying a field along the highway. It couldn't have been a large field — maybe eighty acres. I've watched pilots spray fields many times but today something struck me about their work.

Have you ever noticed how the pilot comes to the end of the field and immediately pulls up, decelerates, banks hard and then zooms directly back to the next strip to be sprayed. He goes in low, accelerates and repeats this process time and time again until his task is finished.

This is the ultimate example of focus. He concentrates on the strip to be sprayed, sprays it and then, wasting little energy and time, banks his plane right back to the field. He doesn't fly to the end of the field then decide to run over to the next section, spray a strip or two, jump to another field then come back to the original field.

Why? He would never get anything accomplished and even if he did he would lose track of where he was on the next field. His efforts would be haphazard — his time would be wasted — and yet isn't that exactly what many of us do every day? We zoom from one field to another, trying to be a jack of all trades and being ineffective in all of them.

Focus. What would happen if we would prioritize our work with a "to do" list and single mindedly concentrate on the task at hand? Then bank our plane at the end of the field and move on to the next one. We'd spray a lot of fields. It takes discipline. We'd have to get organized, use a calendar, be better managers of our time — it's hard work.

Focus. Remember the feeling of satisfaction you've had after seeing a particular task to its completion? Crossing it off of your list and knowing that the day was not wasted? That you really accomplished something?

Focus. Just as a magnifying glass can direct the energy of the sun into a force capable of starting a fire so shall our efforts be — when we focus.

"Destiny is not a matter of chance, it is a matter of choice; it is not a thing to be waited for, it is a thing to be achieved."

— William Jennings Bryan

• • •

Shortly before his death, Sam Walton, founder of Wal-Mart Stores, Inc., was awarded the Presidential Medal of Freedom. President George Bush had this to say in making the presentation: "When Sam Walton's grandchildren read about what makes America great, they'll read about people who have great ideas and great dreams, resourceful people who make imagination come alive with accomplishment. And they'll read about adventurous people who have the drive, ambition and talent to take big risks and to achieve great things."

Was Sam Walton destined to succeed? Was his success a matter of chance? Sam Walton's destiny was a matter of choice — he didn't wait for it — he achieved it. In 1945 he bought a failing Ben Franklin variety store in Arkansas and turned it into the number one franchise in his region. In 1962 he opened his first Wal-Mart. In 1991 Wal-Mart had $44 billion in sales. It is a phenomenal success story — the American dream come true.

I don't believe that Sam Walton was any more intelligent or talented than a lot of people. Like all highly successful people, Walton had a strongly held philosophy. It was a simple philosophy — low overhead, high value and total commitment to the customer. But he lived and breathed that philosophy into the Wal-Mart employees or "associates," as "Mr. Sam" preferred.

Sam Walton had the same opportunity that you and I have. The opportunity to achieve, to risk, to succeed and yes, to fail. The only difference between Sam Walton and most others is that he didn't wait on destiny. He fulfilled his destiny — by choice.

All of us should pay tribute to Sam Walton for showing us that destiny is not a matter of chance but rather a matter of choice. For taking a 5 & 10¢ store in Arkansas and turning it into the world's largest retail company. For showing us that the American dream is alive and well. Thanks Sam, for showing us it can still be done.

"Facts are negotiable, perceptions are not."

— Unknown

• • •

Farm life has really changed over the last fifty years. Rural electrification gave us lights and running water. I remember my mother telling of the miraculous feeling she experienced when she saw water pouring from a faucet indoors after Dad had installed an electric pump and plumbed the house for running water. Until then she had hand pumped water at the well and carried it inside in a galvanized bucket.

Then came rural water districts. Instead of having to rely on the well, rural Americans could have water piped directly to the farm just like their city cousins.

We used to have a farm that was already on rural water when we bought it. Our water pressure was low because we were on the end of the rural water line, according to the previous owners. We accepted this as truth for two years and didn't bother to investigate further.

Then one day we turned on the water only to discover we had excellent pressure. Having never experienced this before we thought it must be a fluke and wouldn't last. But it did.

A month later we once again lost pressure. By now we had grown accustomed to good pressure and we were upset. We now EXPECTED good pressure! I called and asked what the problem was. I was told that a new pump had been installed at the pump station a month earlier but had malfunctioned. It was repaired in a day and we were back up to good pressure once again.

The truth is that we could always have had good pressure — it only required a new pump. For two years we accepted low water pressure as truth because of what other people had told us. We didn't even bother to call about it. If we had only known — we could have had good water pressure all the time.

Perception is truth as far as we're concerned. A perception is like a pump. A faulty perception can cause us to live below our abilities just like a faulty pump can cause low water pressure. Just as our water pressure increased when our pump was replaced, all we need to do is change our perception and we can achieve things in life that we previously considered impossible.

Once our perception is changed we then EXPECT to achieve more. We won't accept going back to a hand pump once we've experienced the power of electricity.

"Facts are negotiable, perceptions are not." Change your perceptions and you'll change your life — that's a fact.

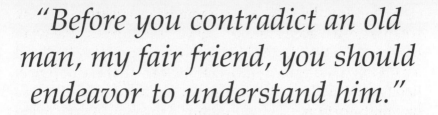

"Before you contradict an old man, my fair friend, you should endeavor to understand him."

— George Santayana

• • •

I have always enjoyed talking to old people. The older I get, however, I'm a bit more careful about who I call old. We in America need to take some lessons from other cultures around the world and hold our elderly in higher esteem. Their experience alone qualifies them as a resource of information to be revered.

Apparently someone decided to do just that — tap into the wealth of knowledge that these senior citizens monopolize. A study was conducted with people over the age of ninety and they were asked this question, "What would you do over in life?" They listed three things — they would have risked more, they would have reflected better and they would have left a contribution to society that outlasted themselves.

They would have risked more. Consider what you are doing in life right now from the perspective of these people who have been right where you are today. When you are ninety plus years old what meaning does risk have? You would realize that life is very short and there is really very little to risk — except life itself. There is no risk after you're dead so it is logical to assume that to risk is to live. Risking is living.

They would have reflected better. If you can reflect on life now as if you are ninety you will make the changes that are necessary for you to achieve the results you desire from life. What you are doing today determines what you will be tomorrow. Taking time to reflect enables you to be objective about yourselves. Objectivity enables you to sort out your undesirable traits and behaviors and enhance your desirable traits and behaviors.

They would make a contribution to society that outlasted them. When Jesus was questioned by his disciples about who would be the greatest in the Kingdom he stated that the greatest must be the servant of all. Imagine again that you are elderly and approaching the end of your life — what will you pass on? Was your life one of giving and serving? Will others say that you made a difference in their lives? Will the lives you have touched be richer or poorer because of the contribution you made?

"Before you contradict an old man, my fair friend, you should endeavor to understand him." History is a harsh critic — it only records actions not intentions.

"A man will remain a rag picker as long as he has only the vision of a rag picker."

— O.S. Marden

• • •

P.L. Gassaway was elected to Congress during the depression years of the 1930s. He was known as the "Cowboy Congressman" from Oklahoma. Always a colorful character, he once rode a horse up the Capitol steps. While campaigning in his district he attended a rodeo. He shocked everyone by peeling off his suit coat, borrowing a horse and entering the steer roping. He took third place. The winner was John McEntire — you may know his granddaughter as country singer Reba McEntire.

But P.L. was not always the famous "Cowboy Congressman." In fact he grew up as the son of a circuit riding Methodist preacher. His father preached among the Indian camps on reservations. But like many in the ministry, they were poor. Another thorn in the flesh for P.L. was his name, Percy Lee — it caused quite a few fights. P.L. only received a second grade education.

But P.L. didn't see himself as only the poor preacher's kid — he had bigger dreams. He was a cowboy by trade but bought a second hand set of law books. He learned well enough to pass the bar exam, set up practice and eventually became a district judge. His crowning achievement was being elected to United States House of Representatives.

Then at the age of fifty he was stricken with a heart attack at his ranch in Oklahoma. Like a true cowboy, he didn't want to die with his boots on — he asked his thirteen year old daughter, Peggy, to take them off. He died in the ambulance on the way to the hospital. Peggy is my mother.

What would posses someone like P.L. to think he could become a congressman when he was a poor, uneducated preacher's kid? It's simple — he didn't see himself as a poor, uneducated preacher's kid. In his mind's eye he saw himself first as a cowboy, then a lawyer, then a judge and ultimately a congressman.

How do we see ourselves? What we see is what we'll be.

"These, then, are my last words to you: Be not afraid of life. Believe life is worth living and your belief will help create the fact."

— William James

• • •

What do you want out of life? What are you doing with your life? Are you living or are you existing? Are you merely trying to get through life to get to retirement? What then? Provoking questions aren't they?

Life is not a spectator sport — life is to be experienced. Why don't we accomplish more, achieve more or more specifically live more? One simple four letter word ... FEAR! We're afraid to live.

Five basic fears turn us into spectators in life instead of participants: Fear of the unknown, fear of change, fear of success, fear of failure and fear of rejection. Overcome these fears and you're on your way to living life to its fullest.

How can you overcome these fears? Ask yourself what the consequences are. Can you accept the consequences of venturing into the unknown — change, success, failure and rejection? To do this requires risk.

William James said, "It is only by risking our persons that we really live at all and often our faith beforehand in an uncertified result is the only thing that can make the result come true." To overcome fear you must master its opposite — faith.

Real living is risky business — it's much like the trapeze artist who asks that the safety net be removed for his triple somersault. To attempt the triple with the net requires no risk. To attempt the triple without a net demands that the flyer face his fears and that takes faith.

Once the trapeze artist completes the triple he experiences a tremendous rush followed by a sense of accomplishment. Now that's really living!

Look back on the experiences in life of which you are most proud. Usually it is a time in which you challenged your fear of the unknown, change, success, failure or rejection. Once you overcame the fear there was a tremendous rush, followed by a sense of accomplishment.

"Be not afraid of life. Believe life is worth living and your belief will help create the fact." Remember, life isn't a spectator sport. Face your fears — take a risk. Have faith — and really live.

"Keep on succeeding, for only successful people can help others."

— Robert Schuller

• • •

I heard the above quote on a broadcast of Dr. Robert Schuller's Hour of Power. It really struck me that, if for no other reason, we should strive to be successful so that we can help other people. He's right — we can't help other people unless we are successful.

One of the Presidential candidates in 1992 was urged by partisan supporters to consider redistributing the wealth in America if elected. In other words tax the wealthiest Americans and redistribute those dollars among the other "not so wealthy." Kind of a modern day Robin Hood.

It's not a new idea. Huey Long, former Senator and Governor of Louisiana, proposed the same idea during the 1930s as a Presidential candidate. It was a bad idea then and it's a bad idea now. Why? Consider the following success story.

Hyrum Smith created the world-renowned Franklin Planner to help people gain control over their lives. Smith says, "Financial success must always be the byproduct of some other success." Ever since he was a young boy he wanted to make a difference. Smith's dream of making a difference is now a reality. He is vice-chairman of the FranklinCovey Co., which trains more than 750,000 people annually.

Redistributing the wealth would put an end to success stories such as this. It would eliminate the incentive to succeed. That will eliminate successful people. Who will we tax then — failures? But more importantly, who will help others succeed?

When people like Hyrum Smith are successful we should stand up and cheer, "Keep on succeeding!" Let's hope the day will never come when we deny anyone the rewards of success — "For only successful people can help others."

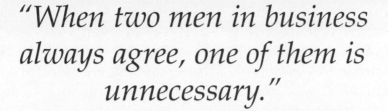

"When two men in business always agree, one of them is unnecessary."

— William Wrigley, Jr.

• • •

There is no sin in disagreement. We tend to think that disagreement creates conflict and that conflict is bad. The opposite is true — disagreement and conflict are desirable and even critical to our own personal growth and the growth of our organization.

Disagreement provides us with a system of checks and balances. This is why our Constitution provides for a balance of power between the executive, legislative and judicial branches of government — and brother do they ever have disagreement and conflict! Without that, however, think how easy it would be to railroad lopsided legislation down the throats of a defenseless public.

The same is true in business — if we surround ourselves with "yes" men and women — we render ourselves defenseless to bad ideas and decisions. There is no one to present the other side of the coin or put the brakes on when the train starts to run away.

As a salesman, one of my bosses was a tough-minded sort who intimidated a lot of our salespeople, even though that was not his intention. He simply "challenged" our thinking. Most would not challenge him in return. This didn't stop me however — we would go at it hard and sometimes disagree fairly violently. When it was all said and done, though, we could shake hands and walk away with no hard feelings. I always admired and respected him for that.

Every organization should strive to create that atmosphere of give and take — one that encourages diverse points of view and mutual respect. Conflict is necessary to deal with change and the only thing that's constant is change. Let's agree to disagree.

"If you aspire to the highest place, it is no disgrace to stop at the second, or even the third place."

— Cicero

• • •

Like you I'm part of a society that's become addicted to instant gratification. Fast food, convenience stores, fad diets — I want what I want and I want it now. Sound like someone else you know?

Patience is a virtue. The problem is that virtues and instant gratification mix like oil and water. A client of mine once said that timing is almost more important than anything. I agree, but what do we do until the timing is right? Let me share a philosophy that I learned as a salesman and still use today. It's simply this, if you can't be in first place make sure you're in second. Why?

In calling on prospects I discovered that many were perfectly happy doing business with their current supplier. I'd thank them for their time, then set about doing two critical things. First, I would call on them as frequently as I could to build a relationship — to let them know that I cared about them even if they weren't buying at the time. The second was this — I'd search for and try to help them solve their most critical problems, even if it didn't have anything to do with what I was selling.

This put me in second place. My other competitors were in third, fourth, or fifth place. I'd have to be patient but eventually the supplier in first place would slip up and make a mistake. Who do you think my prospect would call? That's right, second place Jim, who was about to move up to first. Sometimes it took years but it paid off big time.

The lesson learned is this — assume that the opportunity will come — prepare, pay your dues and be ready. When the timing is right, it will happen. How will you know when the timing is right? You'll know because the people and circumstances will come together to make it a reality. But only if you prepare, you are patient and you believe. You have to believe that good things are going to happen. If you don't, there is no reason to try.

When you can't be first, be second. Be patient — but be ready — then you'll be first.

"Great battles are won before they are actually fought."

— John Lubbuck

• • •

A hospital I was consulting with enlisted teenage volunteers. Several handouts needed to be photocopied and stapled together for a training session we were conducting. The task was assigned to the volunteers. The handouts arrived stapled together haphazardly. I credited the shoddy workmanship to the age of the volunteers.

The more I thought about it though, the sloppiness was not due to youth or even a lack of desire — it was due to the lack of a clearly defined outcome. They didn't know what the end product was supposed to look like.

"People go to work to succeed, not to fail," says Norman Schwarzkopf. Made famous by his role in the Persian Gulf War, "Stormin' Norman" became a role model for visionary leadership. In the case I just shared, the people involved didn't set out to fail. A lack of leadership however, inhibited their success.

Think back to the Persian Gulf War. How was a multi-national military welded into a fighting force so effective that the war was over in a matter of days? Schwarzkopf says the mission was stated so clearly that everyone couldn't help but understand it: "Kick Saddam Hussein out of Kuwait!"

Vision alone isn't enough, however. Here's a quote by Vance Havner that I like: "The vision must be followed by the venture. It is not enough to stare up the steps — we must step up the stairs." After a vision is established and shared, leaders take action. Schwarzkopf's cardinal leadership rule is: "When you are placed in command, take charge!" People can deal with almost anything but uncertainty. They respond to decisive leadership.

Most organizations that I have observed don't suffer from a lack of action. I usually see people working hard. They suffer from a lack of vision. "Action without vision just passes the time," according to futurist Joel Barker. Contrast the Persian Gulf War with the Vietnam conflict. There was plenty of action but no clearly defined purpose or mission. In fact, it frustrated the soldiers, military leaders and the American people.

On the other hand, during the Gulf war, morale was high in the military and the American people responded with a show of support and patriotism unparalleled since World War II.

"Great battles are won before they are actually fought." Sometimes the battle is as simple as getting some handouts photocopied and stapled correctly — sometimes it determines the outcome of an international crisis. In either case, action is only successful if it is preceded by a clearly stated goal or vision, one that anyone can understand. Ask Norman Schwarzkopf — or better yet ask Saddam Hussein.

"Don't eliminate yourself."

— John C. McCollister

• • •

Have you ever been to a conference or a convention and one of the speakers really got your attention? John McCollister was that kind of speaker. His background includes being a former major league baseball pitcher. He has served as Chaplain to the Detroit Tigers and the Detroit Lions. He has authored several books and magazine articles. Dr. McCollister has interviewed celebrities such as George Burns, Ed McMahon, Jay Leno, Jerry Lewis and Phyllis Diller.

In one of his sessions at a writer's conference I attended, he was describing how to find a New York book agent to represent aspiring writers. When one of the participants expressed doubt about being able to pull this off he replied, "Don't eliminate yourself." He explained that you never know unless you try but if you don't try, you'll never know. That's a condensed version of his explanation but you get the meaning.

I attended as many of Dr. McCollister's sessions as I could and visited with him at length. Like all truly successful people he was very open and helpful. He was practical and gave no "pie in the sky" solutions. His teaching was based on years of trial and error.

It occurred to me that his success was due, at least in

part, to his willingness to fail. Why not send a book proposal to an agent or publisher? What's the worst thing that can happen? They might reject it. So what? That's what stops most of us from accomplishing great things. Fear of rejection.

The opposite is what causes people like John McCollister to move on to higher planes of success — they give it a try. If they get turned down, they try again. Eventually, rejection turns into acceptance.

What stands between us and true success? We'll never know unless we give it a try. If we don't try, we've eliminated ourselves.

"That the powerful play goes on and you may contribute a verse."

— Walt Whitman

• • •

Carpe Diem! It's Latin for "Seize the Day." In the film, *Dead Poets Society*, an English instructor in a private boys' school attempts to make poetry relevant. Like most teenage boys they fail to see the value of poetry.

The instructor, portrayed by Robin Williams, leads his students into the hallway during their first day of class and directs them to the trophy case. Enclosed behind glass are the spoils of past victories — photographs, trophies, plaques and citations. The instructor urges them ever closer to the case and asks them to listen carefully. Can they hear anything? It's as if the ghosts from behind the glass are whispering — Carpe Diem — which is Latin for "Seize the Day."

The only time I've recited poetry is in speeches. A verse or two sprinkled in to add a little flavor. In fact, I was looking for such a verse while preparing for a speech in Phoenix and wasn't having any luck. As I do many times when I need to think, I went for a walk — or I intended to. My mind was already out the door and down the drive but my body didn't follow. I found myself standing at a small bridge near our farm in my imagination while I was still seated at the dining room table.

Carpe Diem! I started writing what I envisioned and as I did I found myself standing at another bridge — an overpass on the interstate. I continued to write and by the time I went to bed the poem I had been searching for lay before me. The author was not Kipling or Whitman — it was Whitt. I had written a poem — *A Tale of Two Bridges*. Since then I've written other poems — when I couldn't find one to suit my needs for a particular occasion.

Life, as Walt Whitman describes it, is a powerful play. And what is our role? That we may contribute a verse. Our verse may take many forms other than poetry. The form isn't important. What is important is that we accept the role. To become a participant rather than a spectator. To seize the day!

Participants include those from the past as well as those of us today and will include those in the future. It's a continuing saga and when the accumulative verses of the participants are strung together a certain synergism is achieved. That's what makes the play powerful.

"That the powerful play goes on and you may contribute a verse." I never knew I had a verse to contribute — until I seized the day. Carpe Diem!

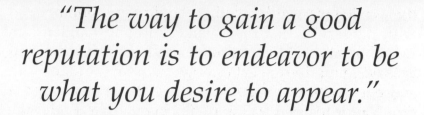

"The way to gain a good reputation is to endeavor to be what you desire to appear."

— Socrates

• • •

When my son Aaron was fifteen, he held down two summer jobs. One as a lifeguard and the other as a busboy in a restaurant.

The restaurant served a seafood buffet on Friday nights — all you could eat. People came from as far as fifty miles away for this Friday night buffet. On Friday nights Aaron greeted and seated people instead of bussing tables. The first night he dressed casually — a sport shirt and jeans. He enjoyed it and got along well with the customers.

I encouraged Aaron to upgrade his wardrobe on Friday nights. After all he wasn't a busboy then, he was the "maitre d'," which by the way, is an abbreviation of the French phrase "maitre d' hotel." Translated that means "master of the house."

The next Friday he put on a nice pair of slacks and a starched long sleeve dress shirt with a tie. He has excellent people skills anyway but his new attire seemed to bring the best out in him. Tips were usually reserved for the waiters and waitresses but people were so impressed with his service that they walked up and handed him money along with compliments on how much they enjoyed his service.

Aaron earned $4.25 an hour but that Friday he earned an additional $7.50 in tips. I commented that his maitre d' image and his excellent service had earned him the equivalent of nearly two hours extra pay.

There are two morals to this story. One is that our image affects both us and our customers. The second is that we add value to our product by giving excellent service — and as Aaron learned, our customers reward us.

"A race horse that can run a mile a few seconds faster is worth twice as much. The little extra proves to be the greatest value."

— John D. Hess

• • •

Peter Vidmar, former Olympic Gold Medalist, says that the difference between winning and losing is very small. He makes the point that to be the best in competition you don't have to be twice as good — the difference between receiving a score of 9.4 and a perfect 10 in an event is a matter of ROV.

ROV is an acronym that stands for Risk, Originality and Virtuosity. In gymnastics that's how judges rate a performance.

Vidmar says that you must be willing to make a really risky move in your routine if you want to outscore the competition. He says you can play it safe, not make any mistakes and look good but not win. To win you must risk something difficult enough to fall flat on your face.

Many gymnasts see a competitor use something

new, then go home to perfect that move. You'll always be one step behind someone else if you adopt that theory however. To win you must come up with something original and unique. According to Vidmar, creativity is the most important part of gymnastics.

Virtuosity, according to the dictionary, is "great technical skill in some fine art." This requires being just a little bit better than the competition. Vidmar says that as parents we often make the mistake of telling our children that they have to work twice as hard as everyone else to succeed in life. This sets an unrealistic goal and proves to discourage rather than motivate. Being a father of four himself he should know.

When training for the Olympics he would practice six hours a day. By working out only fifteen minutes more he calculated that it amounted to an extra month of practice over a year's time. That fifteen minutes only amounts to an additional four percent investment of time each day. A small price to pay for gold — Olympic gold.

"A race horse that can run a mile a few seconds faster is worth twice as much. The little extra proves to be the greatest value." How much of our time are we willing to invest to be a champion?

In business, success is measured by ROI — Return On Investment. Olympic gymnasts measure success by ROV — Risk, Originality and Virtuosity. A little extra ROV equals an ROI that can't be measured in dollars and cents — it can only be measured in gold — Olympic gold.

"I would like to amend the idea of being in the right place at the right time.... You have to recognize when the right time and the right place fuse and take advantage of that opportunity."

— Ellen Metcalf

• • •

When my daughter, Sarah, was eleven years old, she told me that she had a good idea for *The Road Signs For Success Weekly* we publish. That spring we had a tremendous hatch of moths — they were everywhere — hundreds of them. At night they would swarm around the lights. In the morning when we opened a door or window they would flush out in droves.

On one such morning, Sarah opened a window and shooed all the moths out except one stray moth which elected to be difficult. Sarah continually tried to drive the moth out. Finally in frustration she closed the window and the moth was destined to a far worse fate.

The moral, she explained, was this — we should take advantage of an opportunity when we have it because if we don't the window will close. Pretty good insight for an eleven year old.

The moth was in the right place at the right time but failed to see it. Then the window of opportunity closed.

We're not so different from the moth. Our lives contain many windows of opportunities. We fail to see them became we don't look or we're too busy or we just can't believe that the opportunity is for us. It just looks too good or it's too tough or who knows. Then the window closes.

As a salesman, I called on a prospect for seven years without success. Then the window of opportunity cracked open. Because of years of preparation, I was in second place, patiently waiting for the window to open. The window only opened for about two weeks during that seven year stretch. I slipped through the crack, then the window closed. But unlike the moth, I was on the right side. My future was much brighter than his.

Your window of opportunity may be closing. Which side are you on?

"Give me your tired, your poor, your huddled masses yearning to breathe free. Send these, the homeless, tempest tossed to me. I lift my lamp beside the golden door."

— Inscription on The Statue of Liberty

• • •

The 1980s were years of great prosperity in America. Census Bureau figures released in July 1992 revealed median incomes for Americans in 1990. The median income for all households was $30,056, a 75% increase since 1980. Median income means that half of all households brought in more and half less. Unfortunately, good news, like that I just quoted is hidden in a small blurb on page twenty-nine of the daily newspaper. Headlines on the front page scream recession, unemployment and budget deficits.

There's a lot of talk about times being tough during an election year. Challengers for all offices seek to paint a picture of depression and hardship — they say that Americans have the right to be secure. But wait a minute — the census figures say that we had a 75% increase in overall median incomes during the 1980s.

Politicians get elected promising security. Guaranteed jobs, guaranteed wages, guaranteed retirement, guaranteed health care and the list goes on. Our memories are short but we just saw a system with those very guarantees collapse — it was known as communism. The people of the Soviet Union didn't want guaranteed security. They wanted liberty.

The dictionary defines liberty as "freedom from slavery, captivity or any other form of arbitrary control." Security has trade-offs. When someone offers you security, you mortgage a precious piece of collateral — your liberty. The price of security is limitations on your control — someone else calls the shots.

One group of Americans in particular prefer liberty to security. They have the audacity to believe that America is still the "land of opportunity." Many of this group constitute our most recent wave of immigrants — they are a minority — Asian Americans. Median income for Asian Americans was $36,784 in 1990, beating the average by over $6,000. They had the highest median income of any group in the country. Why? Maybe the rest of us have forgotten what all immigrants came to America for. It wasn't security. Many risked their lives to get here. It was liberty. Control of their own destiny. The opportunity to succeed — or to fail — but the choice to do so.

"Give me your tired, your poor, your huddled masses yearning to breathe free. Send these, the homeless, tempest tossed to me. I lift my lamp beside the golden door." Remember it's not called the Statue of Security — it's the Statue of Liberty — and liberty is the only true security that exists.

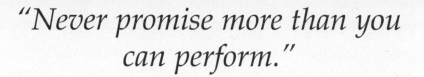

"Never promise more than you can perform."

— Publilius Syrus

• • •

Have you ever been on an airline flight that was over booked? If you have, you'll remember the procedure vividly. Before takeoff, the ticket agent comes on board and makes the announcement that ten more tickets have been sold than there are seats available. The agent then asks for volunteers to give up their seat for a seat on the next available flight, four hours later.

As an incentive they might lure you with a credit entitling you to a $100 discount on your next flight with that carrier. No takers. How about $200? No deal. A round trip ticket anywhere in the continental United States? A few passengers start to stir. A round trip ticket to anywhere in the world? The price is right. People are motivated now. Several passengers rush to claim the prize.

The airline solved their problem, but it cost them money. They had to bribe passengers to pay for their inefficiency. Maybe that's one of the reasons so many have gone bankrupt in recent years.

Those of us with busy schedules tend to be like the airlines sometimes. We over book our lives, then have to bribe our way out of it. How many times have we scheduled more into a day than we could possibly accomplish, then have to either put some people off or, worse yet, forget about them and let them fall through the cracks? How do we feel when that happens? I don't need to tell you.

How much does it cost us not only in business but in relationships with family and friends? We rationalize, of course, but deep down inside we cringe when we have to call the victim of our poor planning and say, "I'm sorry, but ...." Then we go into the weak and illegitimate excuse that we know doesn't hold water.

How do we solve this problem? We have to gain control of our lives through better planning, organization and communication. If our current organizational tools don't serve us well then we need to find others. There are some good ones on the market. If used properly we can dramatically improve our efficiency.

What does it cost us when we over book our lives? The price is always too high.

"A man without a purpose is like a ship without a rudder."

— Thomas Carlyle

• • •

The July 26, 1992 issue of *Parade Magazine* contained a short article entitled "Rethinking Retirement." It reported that a Chicago based out placement firm found that about a third of the older employees who choose early retirement rather than look for a new job regret their decision within the first six months. They often become bored, and miss business and co-workers.

Retirement is something that our society considers the ultimate goal in life. Finally, we don't have to work anymore. Yet statistics show that a high percentage of people die within a few short months of retirement. Why? Because we are naturally goal seeking beings.

Whether we realize it or not we all have goals. As Dr. Denis Waitley puts it, "We are constantly moving toward our most dominant thought." If retirement is that most dominant thought then when we reach retirement age we have no purpose left in life, no reason to live.

I heard Kenneth Blanchard relate a story about Norman Vincent Peale. Blanchard, Peale and Dr. Peale's agent were visiting over supper. The agent asked why Dr. Peale, now in his nineties didn't charge more for his speaking engagements. He could easily command the higher fee and he wouldn't have to speak as often. Why would he want to do that, reasoned Peale, he loved to speak — he didn't want to work less and slow down.

Purpose? Norman Vincent Peale had it and was still enjoying his work in the twilight of his years. Could that be the secret of his long and productive life?

We, like Dr. Peale, should have a purpose that serves as our rudder through life. One that guides us beyond survival or existence, beyond retirement and into a state that makes life meaningful and exciting.

We all have goals — they may be as random as the next thought that pops into our head — there is no sense of direction in that. With that method we are indeed a ship without a rudder — blown by the prevailing wind. Napoleon Hill said, "The only thing we have absolute and total control over is our thoughts." Definiteness of purpose funnels thoughts into a laser beam of power and accuracy.

"A man without a purpose is like a ship without a rudder." We all sail our own ship. Purpose establishes our destination. Without it our course is determined by the most prevalent wind.

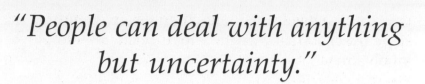

"People can deal with anything but uncertainty."

— Anonymous

•••

I was with a group of clients touring a manufacturing plant. The CEO talked about the people side of the business. He stated that he was particularly proud of the Employee Involvement Program they had implemented where employees participated in teams to implement new ideas. One such idea involved a $300,000 capital expenditure that paid off in seven months. Without employee involvement that wouldn't have happened.

For their book, *The Leadership Challenge,* James M. Kouzes and Barry Z. Posner researched common commitments of leaders that accomplished extraordinary things in organizations. Inspiring a shared vision was one of those commitments.

People can deal with anything but uncertainty. Yet, how many of us are guilty of not sharing the vision with our people? How can we expect people to "buy in" to what we're trying to accomplish if they don't know what the goals and objectives are?

We must have a clearly defined purpose. It must be shared with our people — and it must be communicated with certainty. This gives people a sense of direction —

they can see the destination. Then we need to carry it a step further and ask them to help us get there — employee involvement.

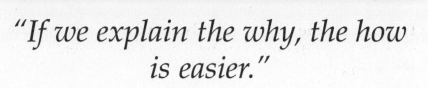

"If we explain the why, the how is easier."

— Jim Whitt

• • •

In our fast lane lifestyles we tend to communicate in what the television and radio media refer to as "sound bites." This is what we see and hear on the evening news. We don't get the whole story but rather a thirty or sixty second edited version of what the news program wants us to see and hear. It is this type of reporting that strikes fear into people who are interviewed on a regular basis — they know that these "sound bites" can distort an entire interview. The whole message gets lost in the editing.

Whether we realize it or not we tend to communicate on a daily basis with family, friends, employees and co-workers in "sound bites." We hurriedly give instructions to someone, rush off to our next project only to return and find that our instructions were "distorted." The receiver of our communication didn't carry out the plan we gave them. This is usually followed by a statement such as, "If you want anything done right, you have to do it yourself." Sound familiar? Maybe, we "edited" part of the message to fit our fast paced format — much like the evening news.

If we would slow down just a little bit we could probably avoid most of these communication breakdowns

— in other words, explain the why behind the how. Why do we want someone to do something a certain way? Without the "why" our instructions may sound picky. The receiver of our message may think of an easier way to perform the task but may inadvertently throw a wrench into the works unless they know the "why" behind the "how."

We've all used the expression, "Do I have to draw you a picture? " The answer is YES — if we want the right results. The "why" paints a picture of the finished result for the receiver — they see what we see — then the "how" becomes easier.

Most people claim that lack of communication is one of the biggest problems in their organization. We can make a big dent in that problem. How? By explaining why.

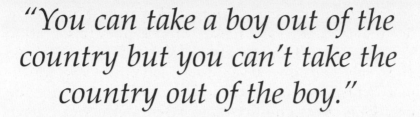

"You can take a boy out of the country but you can't take the country out of the boy."

— Unknown

• • •

America's major cities face major problems. Drugs and crime are taking their toll.

What's wrong? There is much talk today about family values. What are these values? They were once thought of as virtues such as respect for God and country, the institution of marriage, law and order, our elders, the work ethic — virtues taught around the dinner table of rural America.

Now the good news. All is not lost. There is a public school on Chicago's southwest side that has the lowest drop out rate of the city's public schools, one of the highest attendance rates and the enrollment is over eighty percent minority students. Students excel in math and science. Seventy-five percent of the graduates go on to college backed by a scholarship fund of over one million dollars.

It's the Chicago School of Agricultural Sciences. Students learn leadership skills as members of the school's FFA (Formerly Future Farmers of America) chapter. They learn the same things that were taught on the family farm like the work ethic and real environmental conservation — not the kind promoted by radical activists.

What's the moral? Here's my theory. Since the beginning of our country's history, rural Americans have migrated to the cities. They took with them the values they learned back home on the farm or in the small community where they grew up.

Two or three generations later, the descendants of these transplanted rural Americans had no physical connection with their roots. The values once considered sacred were diluted until they no longer had, forgive the pun, any value. The Chicago High School of Agricultural Sciences takes these rural values back to the city and guess what? They still work.

You can take a boy out of the country but you can't take the country out of the boy. But you can take the country to the city and teach a new generation the values that will save their cities.

"Success seems to be largely a matter of hanging on after others have let go."

— William Feather

• • •

The ad was a two page, full color spread. It featured a cowboy standing next to his horse while a blue heeler cow dog sits quietly at his feet. The background was flat prairie strewn with mesquite and sage brush. He looked liked any other cowboy except that he was meticulously dressed — but after all, it was a clothing ad.

The ad copy read like this:

"It's 1979. The music career of a young, Texas cowboy is dead in the water. He decides to quit and design cattle pens.

He talks to his wife. She convinces him to give it just one more year.

Eleven months later, MCA Records signs him up.

Billboard magazine names him its 'New Male Artist of the Year.'

He records twenty-two number one singles. All of

his albums go platinum or gold.

He sells out Madison Square Garden.

Then things really start to take off.

He decides it's good to listen to your wife."

The cowboy is George Strait, country music super-star. As I looked at the ad it reminded me of one of those "What's wrong with this picture?" puzzles. What's wrong is that it should have included his wife. The horse and dog didn't contribute anything to his success. It was her encouragement and willingness to sacrifice that kept him hanging on until he made it.

How many other Texas cowboys could have been country music superstars? Probably quite a few. I'm sure that George Strait would admit he doesn't play a guitar or sing any better than some that peddle their music in thousands of honky tonks every Saturday night.

What's the difference? Why did George make it when others who may have been as talented didn't? A good wife and eleven months. That's it. "Success seems to be largely a matter of hanging on after others have let go." If it weren't for that, someone would be working cattle today in pens designed by George Strait.

"Behavior is a mirror in which everyone shows his image."

— Johann Wolfgang von Goethe

• • •

Most of us rationalize our behavior. Al Capone, the notorious Chicago gangster, stated he simply wanted everyone to have a good time. FBI agent Elliott Ness didn't share that perception. Most would agree that bootlegging, prostitution and murder didn't raise the cultural standards of the windy city during his reign as the king of gangland.

Most of us are not much different from the late Mr. Capone regarding our self-perception, however. There are things we are doing that we know aren't really in the best interest of ourselves or others, yet we can readily explain them away. This is because we have no objectivity when our behavior is in question. We don't see ourselves as others see us. Also, we don't want to admit that we have a problem because that would require us to change. So, we defend ourselves.

One afternoon I discovered that my son, Aaron, had inadvertently recorded over a video of mine while I was away on business one week. His mother had given him permission to use the tape since it wasn't labeled. The video contained a month of programs I had conducted for the Automotive Satellite Television Network in Dallas. I let both of them know in no uncertain terms how I felt about the matter.

Later, after I had cooled off, my wife and I talked about it. She thought I was really out of line. I viewed it differently — I thought I simply expressed my concern in a factual manner. The truth is this — I was hotter than I thought.

I have to work at responding rather than reacting. The biggest problem I have is staring at me in the mirror every morning. That's how it is with all of us — our biggest problems are not external they are internal. It's not someone else, it's me.

"Behavior is a mirror in which everyone shows his image." What do we see in the mirror?

"Change is a two-way street. Either you make it happen or it happens to you."

— Jim Whitt

• • •

Looking out the window of our farmhouse one morning I could see traffic rolling along Interstate 35. The distance between our house and I-35 was roughly the length of three and a half football fields, about 350 yards. What lies in between is a wheat field.

In a year's time thousands of vehicles will pass along that stretch of interstate during which a wheat crop will be sown, harvested and the ground plowed, fertilized and prepared once again for another crop. Change, we've heard it said, is the only constant. That wheat field provides a graphic display of just how true this is.

Change is one of our basic fears. We naturally resist it. It creates stress because it forces us out of our comfort zone. We can reduce this stress, however, by turning the tables on change. We can't avoid change but we can make change happen instead of it happening to us. That means we must look for new and different ways to do things. In other words embrace change, love change, make change happen.

Will Rogers is a great example of an individual who made change happen. He grew up as an Oklahoma cowboy. He went on to perform in wild west shows as a trick roper and eventually vaudeville where he transformed his act into a comedy routine. It made him a star of the famous Zigfield Follies. He then became a star in motion pictures, first silent films and then the talkies.

Will Rogers is probably best remembered as a modern day philosopher. He wrote a daily, syndicated newspaper column where he commented on current events and the political scene. He was an avid supporter of aviation in its infancy and of course it was in an airplane where his saga of change came to an end.

Will Rogers could have resisted change and lived out his life punching cows on the Oklahoma prairie. If he had we never would have known who Will Rogers was. His willingness to embrace change, to make change happen, is what made him famous. It also gave him a marvelously productive and interesting life.

"Change is a two-way street. Either you make it happen or it happens to you." A famous Will Rogers quote was, "All I know is what I read in the papers." The truth of the matter was that he made the news that he read in the papers.

"You can't teach a man anything; you can only help him find it for himself."

— Galileo

• • •

When we think of all the information available to us today we have to wonder why anyone should suffer from a lack of knowledge. We have schools, colleges and universities. We have public libraries where we can check out books, audio and video cassettes or use computers — all for free. Yet, one of the greatest problems facing our nation today is illiteracy — people graduate from high school unable to read.

What's the missing ingredient? It's desire. Teachable people have a desire to learn. They ask questions and they listen to the answers. They find the answers because they want to. They pay the price to obtain the information they desire. Then they use the knowledge because that's the way they really learn, by acting upon the theories they have studied. They make mistakes but figure out a better way to apply that knowledge.

I sum that process up in this simple formula:

DESIRE + COMMITMENT + ACTION = RESULTS

You must have the desire. But that's not enough. You must make a commitment — write it down and tell someone of your commitment, that gives you incentive. Then do it. Your actions are the true test of your commitment. Do this and you will get results.

You cannot teach a man anything; you can only help him to find it for himself. Seek and ye shall find. What is it that you want to learn? Only you can find it.

"Begin with the end in mind."

— Steven Covey

• • •

Colorado enacted legislation requiring high school students to pass a test on the U.S. Constitution, the Declaration of Independence, and the Federalist Papers before they can receive their degree. State Representative Tom Ratterce, who proposed the legislation, supported it on the grounds that "It's important that we know who we are and what we are and how we got there."

I think Representative Ratterce really hit the nail on the head. If we could point to one reason for the major problems our country is facing today it could probably be summed up by saying that we have forgotten who we are, what we stand for and where we are going. Steven Covey, in his book *The Seven Habits of Highly Successful People*, says that we should,"Begin with the end in mind." That's exactly what our country's founding fathers did. Our Constitution answers those three questions.

To be truly successful as an individual, as an organization or as a country you must have a clearly defined purpose. How can you hit a target that you can't see or even describe?

How many of us really know what our country stands for? Those who wrote our Constitution did. We just need to make sure that the torch is passed along or maybe, more accurately, rekindle it for ourselves. The Constitution was written with the end in mind — what our country is supposed to look like and be today.

What about you? Do you have a personal constitution? How about your business or organization? If so, do your employees or members really know who they are, what they stand for and where they are going?

If the answer is no then it's time to rekindle the flame or build a fire if need be. "Begin with the end in mind." No one is going to be very motivated to go anywhere until that destination is clearly established and defined. It's true for our country, your organization and it's true for you.

"A tough lesson in life that one has to learn is that not everybody wishes you well."

— Dan Rather

• • •

My friend Becky Teeter shared a book with me written by Joyce Landorf entitled *Balcony People*. It describes people as either balcony people or basement people. She uses a metaphor comparing life to a glass sphere, much like a fish bowl. In the bottom two thirds of the sphere is dark, murky water. In the top third is clean, fresh air.

The basement people reside in the murk and the mire. They not only are on a dead end street but they insist on trying to pull others down with them. On the other hand, the balcony people live in the clean, fresh air of the upper third, encouraging others to join them. If you're like me you know both groups.

Why do people insist on trying to drag others down? It's because they can't see themselves being on any higher plane than the one they now inhabit. Therefore, they want to level the playing field. So, instead of climbing a mountain of their own, they try to keep us from climbing ours.

They can't do it, however, if we don't allow them. Eleanor Roosevelt once said that no one can make you feel inferior without your permission. The famous First Lady had to overcome plenty of basement people in her life.

On the other hand balcony people constantly encourage us — they provoke us to aspire to loftier heights. I tell people that I am a professional provoker. One definition of provoke is to stir up — another is to excite to action. Balcony people are the affirmers — they tell us that we can do it. They want us to achieve more — to be more successful.

Why do balcony people want us to succeed? Because they are successful themselves. They aren't threatened by our success so they can genuinely encourage us. As far as they're concerned there's plenty of room at the top for everybody.

"A tough lesson in life that one has to learn is that not everybody wishes you well." How about us? Where do we reside? In the basement or the balcony?

"Anyone who strives to be on the leading edge will sometimes be accused of being over the edge."

— Jim Whitt

• • •

Like many college freshmen, I had no idea in the world what I wanted do in life, so I spent my first three semesters as an art major. I had a natural talent but discovered that I really didn't want to spend the rest of my life as an artist — at least in the purist sense of the word. I learned that I could apply the lessons of art to business and life, however.

An artist by the name of Peter Dean describes himself like this: "I'm a magician through whom the images of our time pass and become paintings. I'm an interpreter of reality into fantasy and back again. I'm a juggler of textures and color. I'm a seer of the past and a prophet of the future. I ride the hurricane, I walk the tightrope of sanity. I live on the edge of the world."

Those are the words of someone who is living life to its fullest. Someone who has unshackled his dreams and dares to live "on the edge of the world." The renowned psychologist, Abraham Maslow, would call this self-actualization — reaching our full potential.

To do this we must acquire creative expression. That's what I learned from my stint as an art student. With brush in hand, a palette full of paint and an empty canvas there are no restraints on what we can create — except those that are self-imposed.

A client of mine was mulling over the state of his organization. His dilemma was that he didn't want an organization that was mired in the status quo, yet couldn't help but wonder if some of his ideas were a little crazy. I told him that anyone who is on the leading edge is going to be accused of being over the edge.

Air Force fighter pilots refer to it as "pushing the envelope" — the point at which the pilot has pushed his aircraft to the limits — to where he might lose control. Unfortunately, most people live inside the envelope — and it's sealed. They are trapped by the fear that someone might think they've "gone over the edge."

Life on the edge isn't comfortable. In fact it is downright uncomfortable at times and even scary at others — but it is the way life is intended to be lived. Anyone can be "normal" — any organization can follow the pack.

Anyone who strives to be on the leading edge will sometimes be accused of being over the edge. But those on the leading edge set the pace for the rest of the world.

"It's not people problems, it's people's problems."

— Ward Nairn

• • •

I can walk into any organization and ask them to identify the number one problem that they deal with and invariably the answer will be one of these two — people or communication. Even if the answer is communication, that is a problem with people.

I was visiting with a client one day about this and he coined a phrase I thought was extremely accurate. "It's not PEOPLE problems, it's people's PROBLEMS." What an insight! We talk as though people are the problem. People are the solutions — if you don't think so, try running an organization without them.

Carry it a step further. Customers have problems and it's a good thing they do. If they didn't, we couldn't sell our products and services that help solve those problems. Customers are people, too. It makes no difference what kind of business you're in — you're really in the people business. As a young salesman I was taught the adage that people buy from people, not companies.

Remember what Dr. Norman Vincent Peale said about problems. He made the point that the only people who don't have problems are dead — therefore the more problems you have the more alive you are! Problems are made to be overcome. If we help people solve their problems, we'll solve our people problems.

I have a simple philosophy about building a better business. If you want to build a better business, build a better you. People listen to what you say but they watch what you do. You're the cornerstone of the building. When you decide to become a better person, you will build better people — a solid structure will result — one that won't easily collapse.

It's not people problems, it's people's problems. Let's help people solve their problems, then we'll solve our people problems.

"Make all the money you can. Save all the money you can. Give all the money you can."

— John Wesley

• • •

Hurricane Andrew left in its wake two stories — one of destruction and one of the human spirit under adverse and traumatic circumstances. The first story is one that some estimate is the most devastating and costly natural disaster in the history of America. You saw the video footage on the news — whole neighborhoods leveled, no food or water, people were left homeless and chaos reigned.

What most interested me was people's responses to the situation. Many wanted to know where the government was — why wasn't the government taking care of them? Others pitched in and started helping others — they referred to their neighbors as "family" and set about cleaning up and finding solutions to the problems.

And what about the relief the government was supposed to provide? Military units were dispatched to provide relief in the form of food and shelter and of course they did help.

But it was private citizens either acting on their own

or through church and private relief groups that came to the rescue. They flew in food and clothing on private planes — one even crashed and the passengers were killed — just to help their fellow man. Trucks arrived with so much food and clothing that they had to start turning them away. Hurricane victims refused military food because church groups and other organizations were serving better meals — for free.

When people accuse our nation of being capitalistic and uncaring all they need to do is watch what happens when disaster strikes. It's all of those capitalists who give willingly and generously out of their own pockets to help. This goes on every day even when there is no disaster. Of course, this never makes the evening news. Individuals give to their churches, communities, colleges, charities and directly to individuals.

Why? Because they want to — and they can. You can't give away something you don't have. Think about it — whenever disaster strikes anywhere in the world, who comes to the rescue? It certainly isn't communistic or socialistic nations. They have bankrupted their citizens by taxing away their source of charity — their individual wealth. And no government, including ours, is as caring and generous as the individuals it represents.

We are fortunate to live where free enterprise still drives our economy. John Wesley, the founder of Methodism, understood the value of individual economic freedom when he said, "Make all the money you can. Save all the money you can. Give all the money you can." Wesley knew that you can't give away what you don't have.

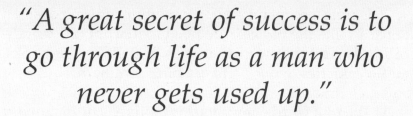

"A great secret of success is to go through life as a man who never gets used up."

— Albert Schweitzer

• • •

Do you ever have that run down feeling? Sounds like an old television commercial doesn't it? It reminds me of a story told by Billy Mayfield of Bay City, Texas.

A man had a car that was getting a few miles on it. It was a good car — it had provided dependable transportation. The problem was that it started using a little oil — a quart had to be added periodically. After a while the man decided that it was just too expensive to keep adding oil to the old car so he decided to stop.

One day as he was driving down the road, the oil light came on and the engine locked up. It was ruined of course. The man crawled out from behind the wheel and scratched his head — he just couldn't understand why the old car didn't hold up.

We tend to be just like the old car. Our little light might be on or our engine might be locked up and we just can't understand why. The reason is simple — we stopped adding oil.

People complain that motivation doesn't last. I agree — like the old car, we need a quart of oil periodically. The oil that we use comes in the form of books, audio cassettes, videos and training seminars.

The root word of motivate is motive. The dictionary defines motive as an inner drive that causes one to act in a certain way. If we're lacking that inner drive then we're probably a little low on oil.

"A great secret of success is to go through life as a man who never gets used up." If we're feeling "used up" maybe we need to add a little oil to our crank case. Then we'll have that inner drive that causes us to act.

"You can never repay the people who help you in your trip through life, but you can pass on the payment."

— Frank Maier

• • •

When I was growing up we had a neighbor named "Doc" Lunsford. I never knew how he came by the nickname "Doc" — his real name was Claude. He had never been a doctor — in fact he didn't even have a grade school education. As a boy Doc had polio and was unable to attend school. He lived with his parents until they both passed away. Doc was probably in his fifties when I can first remember him. He wore bib overalls and lace up *Red Wing* boots. His bout with polio left one leg shorter than the other and he walked with a limp. Doc was thin and had a perpetual five o'clock shadow because he only shaved every other day.

In some ways Doc was totally helpless. He had no car. He walked or had to catch a ride. I can remember Mom tying his tie for him because he didn't know how. She taught Doc how to write his own name. He spent a lot of time at our house and would eat with us often. But Doc was definitely not a taker. He was a giver.

Doc's house was small and it smelled of pipe to-bacco. He didn't have indoor plumbing and he would give me a drink of water with a dipper out of a pail. He always had a bag full of "orange slices," the sugar coated orange flavored candy and he would let me reach in and grab a handful. But most of all I remember Doc's uncon-ditional acceptance of me as a person. Frail looking as he was, he'd pick me up and hug me while scratching his whiskers against my face — that is so vivid that I can still feel it.

Doc could never repay my parents for the kindness they showed him — at least not financially. But I could never repay Doc for the kindness he showed me. If anyone had reason to feel shortchanged in life it was Doc — he never once showed it. Instead he was positive and upbeat — he gave of the only thing he possessed — himself. Doc has since passed on. It's strange but every year around Christmas he always comes to mind. Maybe that's because Doc is what Christmas is all about — unconditional acceptance and giving what is most diffi-cult to give — ourselves.

We can't always repay the people who help us on our trip through life but all of us — no matter what we possess — can pass on the payment.

"Never look back, someone may be gaining on you."

— Satchel Paige

• • •

The banners above the check-out counters caught my eye: "Warehouse of the Year 1988." There was another beside it — same words but a different date, 1989 — then another, 1990, and finally the last was 1991. I was in Sam's Club # 8263, one of Wal-Mart's wholesale clubs in Tulsa, Oklahoma.

"I wonder how this particular warehouse won this award four years running," I thought. Then it occurred to me that a banner for 1992 was missing and this was March of '93 — "I wonder why?" Something else hanging above the check-out counters caught my eye. There were two pieces of poster board hanging side by side. The words were written in freehand with a felt tip marker in pastel colors. Inscribed at the top of the one on the left was a heading, "Motivators in Motion," and following were eight clarifying statements.

My interest was piqued as I moved closer to read each: (1) To do the best we can to make each member feel important. (2) To make daily schedules effective in keeping lines short and checking out quickly and accurately. (3) To run the daily schedule efficiently enough to give all cashiers/callers their breaks and lunch in due time. (4) To show consideration for all cashiers, associates and members. (5) To strive for respect and communication between cashiers, supervisors and management. (6) Strive for accuracy making change at the registers. (7) Strive to make our club the best warehouse and motivate others to do the same. (8) Strive to maintain a positive attitude during stressful situations.

Who were these "Motivators?" Ryan King, cashier supervisor at Sam's told me that the supervisors formed the "Motivators" and developed the eight principles above. Why? "We felt like we had grown complacent," Ryan explained. The missing banner — 1992. It would be easy to point to the banners from '88 to '91 and be content but successful people and organizations don't rest on their past accomplishments.

Satchel Paige pitched in the Negro leagues before professional baseball was integrated when Jackie Robinson broke the color barrier in 1948. He was in the twilight of his career when he finally got to pitch in the majors but was successful even then. When asked for an explanation for his success and longevity he summed it up like this, "Never look back, someone may be gaining on you." That's a philosophy that Satchel Paige, the "Motivators in Motion" and all truly successful people have in common.

"Every noble work is at first impossible."

— Thomas Carlyle

• • •

We live in a time when the majority of Americans enjoy the highest standard of living known to man. This has created a problem that has actually caused us to regress — complacency. We are too comfortable. We have evolved into a nation of security seekers.

There are still people who take a risk and make it, however. In an issue of *Inc.* magazine, the cover story dealt with successful companies that were started with $1,000 or less. Most of the companies cited were started within the last ten to twenty years. Most had sales in the millions.

How do these people do it? People who accomplish the seemingly impossible usually posses one common trait — they have great faith. They believe they can do it and they do.

A great example of faith is portrayed in the movie *Indiana Jones and the Last Crusade.* Indiana, in pursuing the Holy Grail, passes through a series of three tests to reach the prize. After passing the first two he finds himself at the edge of a great chasm with no way to cross and thousands of feet to fall to the bottom. He is instructed to take the leap of faith and finally musters the courage to step off the ledge. He falls — but only about a foot below he lands on a rock bridge that is camouflaged. He couldn't see it until he stepped out. That's what faith is — you can't see it until you step out.

Speaking of Indiana, I became acquainted with a man by the name of Steve Toskos in Fort Wayne. Steve and his wife, Mae, came to this country from Greece in 1960. Steve wanted to buy a business he became interested in, Greenblatts Furs. He had no knowledge of the business but approached Mr. Greenblatt about buying the business. He had no money so he worked as a mechanic. It took twenty years of hard work and saving but Steve and Mae realized their dream. As Steve told me this story in his heavy Greek accent I had to admire the quality that carried him — faith. Just like Indiana Jones, he stepped out — and when he did the bridge was there.

"Every noble work is at first impossible." Have faith — but remember — you can't see it until you step out.

A Personal Note

I like the way H.G. Wells, the famous British author, defined success: "Wealth, notoriety, place and power are no measure of success whatever. The only true measure of success is the ratio between what we might have been and what we might have done on the one hand and the thing we made and the thing we made ourselves on the other." In other words, how close are we coming to reaching our full potential?

It is my sincere desire that the signs contained in the pages of this book will guide you on the road to reaching your full potential.

About the Author

Jim Whitt is a professional provoker! He provokes people to challenge what they do, why they do it and how to change it. His purpose in life is "to help people reach their full potential." His vehicles for fulfilling that purpose are writing, speaking and consulting.

Raised in the cattle country and oil fields of Oklahoma, Jim worked as a cowboy and then became a top producing salesman and marketing executive with two Fortune 500 companies. Armed with a degree in animal science, he uses "Cowboy Psychology" to help people understand the principles of human motivation. Jim is a dynamic and entertaining speaker. His presentations are punctuated with his unique brand of humor that draws on his experiences as a cowboy and feed salesman. Imagine Will Rogers as a management consultant and you've got a picture of Jim Whitt on the platform.

Today Jim and his wife, Sondra, are partners in a management consulting firm and are founders of *The Institute for Purposeful Living*, a nonprofit organization that helps people discover their purpose in life.